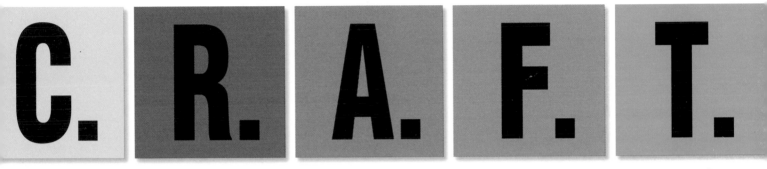

C. R. A. F. T.

CREATING REALLY *awesome* FREE THINGS

100 SERIOUSLY FUN, SUPER-EASY PROJECTS FOR KIDS

JAMIE DOROBEK, Creator of **C.R.A.F.T.**

Adamsmedia
Avon, Massachusetts

DEDICATION

To my sweet Maxwell, for your inspiration to write this book. I love you more than the moon and the stars and the sun and the sky! And to my Mom for encouraging and inspiring my creativity as a child. I love you, Mom!

Published by
Adams Media, a division of F+W Media, Inc.
57 Littlefield Street, Avon, MA 02322. U.S.A.
www.adamsmedia.com

ISBN 10: 1-4405-9168-7
ISBN 13: 978-1-4405-9168-6
eISBN 10: 1-4405-9169-5
eISBN 13: 978-1-4405-9169-3

Printed in the United States of America.

10 9 8 7 6 5 4 3 2 1

Library of Congress Cataloging-in-Publication Data
Dorobek, Jamie.
  Creating really awesome free things / Jamie Dorobek, creator of C.R.A.F.T.
    pages cm
  Includes index.
  ISBN 978-1-4405-9168-6 (pb) -- ISBN 1-4405-9168-7 (pb) -- ISBN 978-1-4405-9169-3 (ebook) -- ISBN 1-4405-9169-5 (ebook)
1. Handicraft. 2. Handicraft--Equipment and supplies. 3. Household supplies. I. Title.
  TT157.D6375 2015
  745.5--dc23
                    2015025899

Readers are urged to take all appropriate precautions before undertaking any how-to task. Always read and follow instructions and safety warnings for all tools and materials, and call in a professional if the task stretches your abilities too far. Although every effort has been made to provide the best possible information in this book, neither the publisher nor the author is responsible for accidents, injuries, or damage incurred as a result of tasks undertaken by readers. This book is not a substitute for professional services.

Many of the designations used by manufacturers and sellers to distinguish their products are claimed as trademarks. Where those designations appear in this book and F+W Media, Inc. was aware of a trademark claim, the designations have been printed with initial capital letters.

Cover design by Erin Dawson.
Cover and interior photographs by Jamie Dorobek, Sarah Schiffman, and Erin Dawson.
Interior illustrations @ Roman Sigaev, pzaxe, 1enchik, and artishokcs/123RF.

This book is available at quantity discounts for bulk purchases. For information, please call 1-800-289-0963.

ACKNOWLEDGMENTS

I have precisely one billion people that I need to thank for helping me complete this book. First and foremost my husband, Andy: Thank you for not only happily embracing the giant craft tornado that blew through our house for seven crazy weeks, but for cheering me on every step of the way. Thank you for doing way more than your fair share of the dishes, bath times, and bedtimes so that I could work on this wild book at night. Thank you for being an amazing father, and for being the perfect life partner for me. I love you more than you know.

To my parents, thank you for showing me that hard work, dedication, and being a nice human pays off. Thank you for allowing me the freedom as a child to glue plastic Hawaiian leis to my lamp shades even though it wasn't your style. Thank you for embracing my creativity and for loving me always.

To Sarah Schiffman, thank you for coming over not once, not twice, but on four separate occasions to chase kiddos around my backyard and take beautiful action shots of kid crafts for this book. Your skills as a photographer are out of this world, and your generosity and kindness as a human are even more admirable.

To Amy, Annie, Courtney, Jennifer, Kelly, Rachel, Tanner, Taylor, Terri (my mom again), and Vanessa: I am forever grateful for your craft and photo contributions to this book. I love that this book is a collaboration of some of the most creative people I know.

Thank you Katie for editing my madness. Thank you Christine for being the best cheerleader ever. Thank you Frances for your great legal advice. Thank *you* for buying my little ol' book. And last but not least, a giant bear hug thank you to all of the people who have been interested in my ideas and words on *C.R.A.F.T.* for the past five years. This book would have never been a possibility without y'all!

CONTENTS

Chapter 4: BATHROOM 127

Chapter 5: GARAGE 165

Chapter 6: NATURE 191

INTRODUCTION

DID YOU KNOW that you can make monster feet out of tissue boxes? A sheep out of a ziptop bag and some shredded paper? A watch for dress-up out of an empty toilet paper tube?

Creativity is contagious, and throughout *Creating Really Awesome Free Things* you'll find 100 fun and easy kid crafts that teach you how to use what you have to make some super-fun free things! I came up with most of these crafts on my own (I'm a mom, craft blogger, and former teacher, so creativity is my middle name), but you'll find some contributor projects scattered throughout the book as well. I hand-picked each contributor because I love his or her individual sense of style and perspective on kids in general. Most of the contributors have kids—and two are actually kids themselves. But no matter who came up with the craft, each project is pretty much free!

So what do I mean when I say "free"? Well, the projects in this book are made up of items that you most likely already buy and will have on hand. Think water bottles, cotton balls, tape, and rubber bands. So by free, I really mean one of two things: (1) You will use the packaging of an item you most likely already buy (such as cereal boxes or egg cartons) or (2) you will use the actual contents of an item that you probably already have on hand (such as cotton swabs, permanent markers, and sandpaper). Make sense? I want you to feel empowered by the idea that you already have all of the fanciest kid crafting supplies at your fingertips. There is no need to go out and buy special things. And, to make it easy for you to find your amazing "free" crafting materials, the book is divided up by rooms in your house. Why waste time searching for materials when you can be crafting with your kids!

In addition to the crafts, you'll find a chapter full of information about what you should save from the recycling bin (candy wrappers, magazines, tin cans), what you probably already have on hand (string, coffee filters, paper plates), and what basic craft supplies you'll find yourself using over and over again (glue, paint, hole punch). Throughout the book, you'll find Keep It Creative! sidebars that give information on project variations and alternatives. And you'll also find Awesome Fact sidebars containing trivia about the animal, topic, or item a craft is themed around; these are designed to help you inspire a love of learning in your kids and spark conversations that will continue long after you're done crafting.

The majority of the crafts in this book can be 100 percent completed by preschool-age or elementary school–age kids—but you know your kids best, so let them do whatever they can, and be available to help them out with the rest! A few of the crafts utilize materials that will absolutely need adult supervision, including a hot-glue gun, utility knife, and drill (and one—really awesome—craft actually needs a corkscrew), so just be sure to read through the instructions before starting a project.

I promise you will have fun crafting with your kids, and you might even want to get in on the fun. The Macaroni Necklace in Chapter 3 can really spruce up a plain tee and a pair of jeans—just saying! So get ready to rifle through your home office, clean up your kitchen, and even spend some time collecting materials in your own backyard as you start creating a bunch of really awesome free things with your kids.

Chapter 1

WHERE TO START

So you want to start crafting, but what should you have on hand? Where does all this "free" stuff come from? This chapter will ensure that you and the kids are ready for spontaneous craft sessions whenever inspiration hits.

Here you'll find a variety of information on the various materials that will let you make all 100 kid craft projects in this book. You'll also find ideas for alternative materials just in case you don't have something that a project calls for. For example, if you don't have paint stir sticks that are needed to complete a project, you can easily swap those out for chopsticks, Popsicle sticks, or even twigs from nature! I've also included some fun ideas on how to make crafting with kids a little less messy, slightly more organized, and . . . you guessed it . . . free!

Items to Save

Now, I don't want to encourage you to be a hoarder, but I do want you to consider saving a few everyday items from the trashcan or recycling bin. I'm all about practicality, and no one has room in her house to store every egg carton and plastic milk container she's ever used. My solution? I keep one small cardboard box that is about 20" × 14" stored in the garage, and fill it with items to save for crafting. I typically use one of those economy size diaper boxes, since they are so readily available in my house! This keeps my hoarding to a minimum and the free craft supplies flowing! But what exactly should you hold on to? These items include the following:

Plastic Food Containers

This category includes items such as plastic milk jugs, yogurt containers, baby formula containers, and water bottles. Empty water bottles will magically turn into polar bears, milk cartons will be turned into sun catchers to make your windows sparkle, and baby formula containers also make really great drums when paired with chopsticks! In this book, you'll use gallon milk jugs and 16-ounce, plastic water bottles for multiple crafts.

KEEP IT CREATIVE!

Crafting with what could be considered trash is also a great way to talk to kids about the three R's: Reduce, Reuse, Recycle! Things like egg cartons, plastic food containers, and cereal boxes are some of the very best craft supplies a kid (or parent) could ask for!

Egg Cartons

You'll find that egg cartons come in handy in any number of ways. They are the basis for the Egg Carton Camel and Egg Carton Flowers in Chapter 2 and they are fantastic when used as paint pallets for kids—especially when a project calls for a variety of different colored paints! Just pour a little bit of each paint color into each egg indent and you have an inexpensive, mess-free way to keep your kids' creativity flowing. Then, once the project is finished, you can just toss the egg carton, making clean up a breeze as well!

Cardboard Food Boxes

This category includes items like cereal boxes, the boxes for frozen foods, and cracker boxes. Cardboard food boxes make the perfect blank art canvas for kids. They are sturdy enough to be painted on, but also easy enough to cut with a simple pair of scissors. To store these, use your finger to rip the seams on the side and on the bottom so that the box lies flat. I keep at least ten empty, flat food boxes in my garage stash. If you don't have cardboard food containers on hand, you can typically replace these with notecards, card stock, brown paper bags, the fronts of notebooks or folders, or even plain white printer paper.

Tin Cans

Lots of food comes in tin cans and you probably just throw these in the recycling bin after you pour out the green beans, spaghetti sauce, or soup. But those tin cans can provide hours of fun, so keep some clean ones stored in your craft bin! For most of the projects in this book, it's ideal to use a 16-ounce or 18.6-ounce soup can, but you can absolutely substitute whatever size tin can you have on hand. If you don't have tin cans in your stash for a project, feel free to use an empty glass jar or even a plastic food container, such as a yogurt container.

Depending on the craft, you might not need to worry about removing the label from the tin can. But there are a few crafts where that is necessary and I will make that clear on a project-by-project basis. If you do have to remove the label, don't worry! This is typically pretty easy. I like to remove as much of the label as possible when the tin is dry. Then, rinse the can out, and use

warm water to remove the remaining part of the label. If a label doesn't want to come off, just soak the can in hot, soapy water for 15 minutes, then peel. Don't worry if you don't get every last bit of label off.

Brown Paper Bags

Much like a cardboard food box, a brown paper bag makes for an awesome blank canvas that is easy to manipulate with scissors—and best of all, they are free from most grocery stores! For all of the projects in this book we will use large brown bags from the grocery store. Feel free to substitute with brown kraft paper that comes in packages or even small lunch-size brown bags, if needed.

Candy Wrappers

You'll use candy wrappers for a few projects throughout the book, so when the time comes to have a treat, save the wrapper for a rainy day and craft up a few Candy Wrapper Bow Barrettes or a Pencil Bag, both crafts in Chapter 3! You will want to carefully open the candy wrappers so that when you are ready to craft, the wrapper will be fully intact! If you don't have candy wrappers available, feel free to use a section from the front of a magazine cover. Even a page from the Sunday comics would be a colorful alternative.

Magazines

By "magazine," I mean any thin, shiny paper with patterns, pictures, or letters. You can save regular magazines, mail order catalogues, or the coupon foldouts that you get in the mail. You'll use magazines specifically to create a snail mail Envelope and a Paper Bead Necklace, both found in Chapter 3. But magazines can also come in handy to jazz up a variety of crafts. You can use magazines as an alternative to construction paper or tissue paper as well. In the Monster Feet craft in Chapter 4, I used mostly blue pages from a magazine to spiff up tissue boxes. Add three magazines to your box in the garage and you should have enough to see you through any craft you choose to do!

Toilet Paper Rolls

Toilet paper rolls will get new lives throughout the book as a watch, a bracelet, five different animals, and a lighted garland. All of these projects are found in Chapter 4. A plus is that toilet paper rolls and paper towel tubes can be used interchangeably! In this book, I say to use toilet paper rolls or tubes, but paper towel tubes can easily be cut in half and used the same way.

Household Items

Along with recycled items, you will find a variety of typical household items such as cotton balls, string, and wooden clothespins used in the projects throughout the book. Again, if you don't have these items on hand, don't worry about it! Use what you have and save your money for more critical needs. Here are a few of the household items you may find yourself searching for.

String

When a project calls for string, you can use thin leather scraps, string, yarn, skinny ribbon, baker's twine, or elastic. For the majority of the projects in this book you will not need more than 60" of any one kind of string. (The String Obstacle Course in Chapter 6 is the exception.) So start saving those 5"-plus scraps of all things stringlike! Gifts are a great place to find "free" small pieces of ribbon to add to your craft stash.

Clothespins

I use wooden clothespins in my kitchen to secure cereal, chip, and pasta bags, so I always have them handy. In this book, they are used as giraffe legs, as paintbrushes, and even as a simple way to display printed pictures and art. I also like to use clothespins as small clamps. For instance, if you are gluing cardboard owl eyes to a paper plate, just grab two clothespins and use them to hold the owl's eyes to the paper plate so you don't have to waste another second of crafting due to drying time! Then simply unclamp.

Coffee Filters

Coffee filters are one of my very favorite crafting canvases. Kids (and adults) love watching the tie-dye effect in action when the water hits the marker on the coffee filter. If you don't drink drip coffee, don't worry—you can grab a pack of 100 coffee filters from the store for less than a dollar! You could also nicely ask your office or neighbor if you could have a few for craft purposes. I have a feeling they wouldn't turn you down.

Paper Plates

White paper plates are my favorite, but don't fret if all you have is leftover *Frozen* paper plates from your daughter's birthday party. Paint is your friend! Or check to see if the back side of the paper plate is white, and just use that side as the front. Some crafts call for thin paper plates while others work better with a heavy-duty paper plate; I've noted what plates work best for which projects throughout the book. But if you don't have heavy-duty paper plates on hand, just put 2 or 3 thin ones together with glue! Also, if you don't have any paper plates available, consider just using white cardstock, an empty food container box, or cardboard cut into a circle.

Tape

Tape is such a versatile crafting tool! There are many kinds of tape, including clear tape, masking tape, painter's tape, packing tape, duct tape, electrical tape, and washi tape. All of these kinds of tape will be utilized to make crafts in this book. But if you don't have a certain kind on hand, you can absolutely substitute for whatever kind you do have. For instance, washi tape is not as common in many households, so think about using permanent markers to doodle on white masking tape to give it the same colorful look without going to the store! Another modification is to use construction paper, magazine cutouts, or glitter underneath clear packing tape. This will spruce up your plain tape in no time.

Permanent Markers

Permanent markers, such as Sharpies, come in a variety of colors and are perfect for writing and drawing on a variety of surfaces. A black permanent marker is crucial for making kid crafts in this book. If you don't have one on hand, this is one thing I would say you have to buy. Sorry! For some of the crafts in this book, you can substitute other kinds of markers or paint for permanent markers. But you will need permanent markers for a few of the crafts, including Tie-Dye Shoelaces (Chapter 3), Faux Stained Glass (Chapter 3), and the Ribbon Wand (Chapter 4).

Notecards

As a retired teacher, I have a ridiculous amount of note-cards still on hand because they were invaluable as flashcards for students. However, you can replace notecards with card-stock or even plain white printer paper if you don't have any on hand. I do love that notecards are a pre-cut size (and any size notecards will work for the projects in this book) and have lines to help guide measurements and handwriting!

Rubber Bands

Rubber bands will be used to decorate the Rubber Band Desk Organizer (Chapter 3) and to turn twigs into Stars (Chapter 6). If a project calls for rubber bands, any kind of elastics will work, even hair ties. While I only specifically used rubber bands in two crafts, you can absolutely use these crafting gems in a variety of other ways, including as bristles for the Texture Painting in Chapter 6 or in some instances to replace string.

Cotton Swabs

Cotton swabs (I like to use the Q-Tip brand) make the perfect tiny paintbrushes for painting small details. We will be creating a pointillism-inspired art piece and making details in a cactus painting with cotton swabs in this book, both in Chapter 4. And if you are out of cotton swabs, no worries—you can always substitute the eraser end of a pencil. You could also use cotton swabs to replace cotton balls or shredded paper as filler for the Water Bottle Polar Bear (Chapter 4) and Ziptop Bag Sheep (Chapter 3).

Cotton Balls

Throughout the book, you'll find cotton balls turned into Sushi (Chapter 4), used as a filler to make a Water Bottle Polar Bear (Chapter 4), used as the bristles for a clothespin paint-brush in Texture Painting (Chapter 6), and more! You probably already have cotton balls in your bathroom, but if you don't, you can substitute white shredded paper or even newspaper. Another great substitution for cotton balls is batting, foam, or the insides of bed pillows—really, anything white and fluffy will work perfectly!

Paint Stir Sticks

Every time you buy a gallon of paint they hand you a few stir sticks, and if you're like me you have quite the collection lingering on a shelf in the garage! Throughout the book, you'll see how these can be turned into everything from a tic-tac-toe game to plant markers (see projects in Chapter 5). Depending on the craft, paint stir sticks can be switched out for a variety of other sticks, including chopsticks, Popsicle sticks, 12" rulers, wood shims, or sticks and twigs that you can find in your own backyard!

Basic Craft Supplies

In addition to the recycled items you'll use to make the crafts throughout the book, you will also need to have a few basic craft supplies on hand. And I want to continue to arm you with a list of substitute supplies so you can get creative with the things you already have in your home. In most cases, there is no need to go and buy something new.

Glue

You will see glue in the materials list for a lot of projects in this book. I typically use Elmer's glue products. They're washable, nontoxic, and easy to clean up! Many types of glue will work for the crafts in this book, including glue spots, glue sticks, scrapbook-style tape runners, and even a hot-glue gun. If you don't have glue on hand, tape is a great alternative.

Decoupage Medium

Mod Podge is a brand of really thinned out glue and sealer for decoupage projects. If you have actual Mod Podge on hand, awesome! If not, it's very simple to make something similar with things you likely already have. Just empty 1 bottle of Elmer's School Glue into a clean plastic food container. A clean empty butter or yogurt container with a lid works great. Then, fill the glue bottle with water, shake it so any leftover glue is mixed in, and pour into the plastic container that holds the glue. Stir the water and glue together until the glue has been completely mixed into the water and the water is a milky white color, about 5 minutes, then use with any paintbrush. Be sure to store it with a lid on so that it does not dry out.

Colored Paper

You'll find colored paper used in many of the projects throughout the book where it's cut, folded, glued, hole-punched, and more. If a project calls for colored paper, the best thing to use is construction paper. It comes in many colors and is inexpensive. But if you and your kids are sitting down to start a project and you don't have construction paper on hand, feel free to use white paper colored with markers, magazine pages, scrapbook paper, tissue paper, or anything else that you can think up.

Paint

Where would kids' crafts be without paint? You and your kids can use brushes, cotton swabs, leaves, your hands, and many other objects to put this medium on the page, rock, etc. I love to use Crayola Washable Kids' Paint because it covers well, comes in a nice range of colors, and, most important, cleans up easily! But you'll find a few projects throughout the book that specifically call for acrylic paints instead. You'll find the paint for these projects called out in the materials lists, but if you don't see that designation, feel free to use whatever type of paint you have in the house. And if your paint supplies are running low, you can give these projects a splash of color by using permanent or other kinds of markers, crayons, colored pencils, paint pens, or colored paper instead.

Paintbrushes

When it comes to applying paint, there are many different kinds of paintbrushes you can use. But for the kids' crafts in this book it really isn't going to make much difference if you use a sponge brush or a bristle brush. Just use whatever you have on hand. Fingers work well too! For the Altered Scrapbook and the Sandcastle Magnets, a 2" sponge brush would make the painting process go a little faster, but don't worry if you don't have one in the house.

Also, I usually just use one paintbrush per project and rinse the paintbrush out at the kitchen sink in between colors. This makes clean up at the end of the craft a little easier. If you don't want to take the time to do this, consider using one paintbrush per color of paint. It's totally up to you!

Writing Utensils

Markers, crayons, colored pencils, paint pens, colored pens: All of these coloring devices are fair game in kids' crafts! Some crafts will specifically call for crayons or permanent markers, but if you do not see that designation, feel free to use whatever you have on hand.

Single-Hole Punch

A single-hole punch is a very important crafting tool that is likely hiding in your office nook/room/cabinet right now. Hunt it down! A hole punch makes the perfect tiny circle for the eyes of a creature or even to assist in stringing a dream catcher.

Hot-Glue Gun

In adult craft world, the hot-glue gun is your best friend. With kid crafts, I have tried my best to limit the use of the hot-glue gun, but there are a few crafts that just need a little more than Elmer's glue, such as the Candy Wrapper Bow Barrettes in Chapter 3 and the Flip Catch game in Chapter 5. There are other crafts where the hot-glue gun is not essential but would make things move along more quickly and easily— for instance, when gluing paint stir sticks to paper plates to make masks, props, or puppets. You could use packing tape, but the hot-glue gun would be the fastest and sturdiest method in that situation. It's important to be safe, but you know your kids best so let them do as much as you feel comfortable with and help them with the rest!

Let's Get Started!

As you can see, there's no reason to let the materials lists for each project get in the way of your kids' creative genius— and there's no reason to run out to the store to buy materials whenever you decide you want to do something fun. If you don't have something on hand, turn the challenge into an opportunity to come up with an alternative and keep on crafting! At least for me, crafting with kids is all about the creative process, not the actual product. The actual product is fun too, but the process of trial and error and problem-solving is a great life lesson. Try not to let your kids get caught up in making their craft look exactly like the picture. Instead, encourage them to be creative with color, texture, supplies, and design. Creativity is contagious—pass it on!

Chapter 2

KITCHEN

Your kitchen is full of food, appliances, plates, silverware, pots, pans—and craft supplies. You don't think so? Well, cereal boxes make awesome gift bags and also serve as blank canvases for a variety of crafts throughout this chapter (and the book as a whole), including a puzzle. Brown paper bags from the grocery store are pure gold in the world of kids' crafts, and here you'll find a variety of clever uses for them including a cowboy vest and a drum. Leftover paper plates from last year's barbecue? Perfect! You'll find a slew of clever things to make, like the Pizza Pocket, Panda Mask, and Ring Toss—and the Paper Plate Owl always proves to be a big "hoot" with the kids. So, what are you waiting for? Get in your kitchen and start crafting!

Pizza Pocket

Pizza is always a winner in our house, and this craft allows kids the creativity to put absolutely anything they want on their very own paper pizza. Pepperonis? Mushrooms? Pineapple? Or how about gummy bears and broccoli pizza? This pizza craft pulls double duty, and not only serves as an ode to a favorite food but also allows your kids to keep special treasures close in their pizza pockets!

Paintbrush
2 heavy-duty paper plates
Paint (I used brown, red, and orange)
Pencil
Scissors
Colored paper (I used yellow, red, black, and green)
Hole punch
Glue
Stapler
24" of ribbon

1. Use a paintbrush to paint the back of 1 paper plate red. Don't worry if the red does not completely cover the rim of the paper plate.

2. Allow the paint to completely dry according to package instructions, then flip the plate over and use a pencil to draw a triangular slice of pizza onto the plate. I made my slice about 5" wide at the top. Next, use your scissors to cut the triangle out of the red paper plate. This will be the slot to take things in and out of your pocket.

3. After your paper plate is completely dry, paint the outside rim of the red paper plate brown to mimic a pizza crust. Then paint the front and back of the second paper plate your favorite color. This will be the color that shows on the inside of your pizza pocket. I chose orange!

4. Use colored paper to cut out the pizza toppings. You can use mine as an example, but get creative! I used large red circles for pepperonis, smaller green circles for jalapeños, skinny yellow rectangles for cheese, and black circles with a hole punched in the center for olives.

5. Glue the pizza toppings to the red paper plate. Don't be afraid to let your pizza toppings overlap!

6. To make the pizza pocket's handle, staple the ribbon to the left-hand top of the red paper plate, close to where the pizza pocket was cut, and then to the right side of the same paper plate.

7. Finally, sandwich your 2 plates together with the bottoms of each plate facing outward. To secure your pizza pocket, staple the paper plates together with 6–8 additional staples around the plates.

Awesome Fact

Some popular pizza toppings in Japan are squid and Mayo Jaga, which is just mayonnaise, potato, and bacon. Who knew?

Emoji Photo Props

In case you're new to the emoji world, emojis are digital icons used in electronic messages to show, well, emotions. The little yellow faces are popping up all over our phones and messages! These photo props are fun to make, and even more fun to play with. After the kids make a few Emoji Photo Props, encourage them to do a silly photo shoot! Send pictures to friends and family via text— and don't forget to add the corresponding emoji!

Paintbrush
1 heavy-duty paper plate per photo
  prop you want to make
Yellow paint
Scissors

Colored paper (black and red)
Glue
Tape
1 paint stir stick or chopstick per
  paper plate

1. Paint the top side of each paper plate yellow. Allow to dry according to package instructions.

2. Use scissors to cut 2 (3") oval-shaped eye holes out of each paper plate. The eye holes do not need to be perfect.

3. Cut emoji features—eyes and mouths—out of black and red paper, being sure to line up the eye holes correctly. Note: Black construction paper is way easier to cut than the heavy-duty paper plate and will hide any imperfections of the eye holes cut in the paper plate.

4. Glue the faces onto your paper plate.

5. Use tape to add a paint stir stick or chopstick to hold your photo prop.

KEEP IT CREATIVE!

To line up the eye holes, use a straight edge of a ruler, book, or envelope to draw 2 lines. One line will be the highest part of the eye hole and one line will be the lowest part of the eye hole.

Paper Plate Owl

It seems that toys, shows, and pictures featuring woodland animals are everywhere you look! And if your child is in love with all things owl, then this is the project for you. All you need is a single paper plate, a cereal box, and a few other basic materials that you probably already have in your home to make this adorable owl. Once your owl is dry and ready to go, have your kids create a nest for the owl with sticks and leaves from the backyard. It's guaranteed to be a hoot!

1 thin paper plate
Paintbrush
Paint (I used orange)
1 cereal box
Scissors
Glue
2 sheets of colored paper (I used yellow and orange)
Black marker

1. To make the owl's wings, fold the sides of your paper plate toward the center of the plate. You don't want the wings to touch; you want to have enough space to craft the owl's belly. Then, to make the owl's head, fold the top of the paper plate down about 2".

2. Paint the owl's wings orange. Allow the wings to completely dry per package instructions.

3. Disassemble your cereal box by gently ripping the seams on the side and bottom of the box with your finger. Then, cut different-size ovals out of a cereal box and glue each one to the owl's belly. It's fun to have a variety of sizes; my ovals range in size from ½" to 2" wide and 1" long. To give the owl's belly some added interest, glue the blank or the colorful side of the cereal box ovals to the belly so that the words and the design of the cereal box show.

4. Cut 2 silver dollar–size circles for eyes and 2 (2"-long) feet out of yellow colored paper, then cut a 1" triangle out of orange colored paper for the beak.

5. Glue the beak to the center bottom of the owl's head, and then glue the two eyes centered on top of the beak so that they overlap just a little bit. Glue the feet to the backside of the bottom of the paper plate. Then use a black marker to draw the owl's pupils onto the eyes.

Awesome Fact

Did you know that owls have three eyelids?: One for blinking, one for sleeping, and one for keeping the eye clean.

Panda Mask

This super-cute panda mask is the perfect addition to the dress-up drawer or even as part of a Halloween costume. All you will need in addition to the panda mask tutorial below is a black T-shirt and black pants. Then, just cut out a white circle of felt and safety-pin it to the black T-shirt. Voilà—panda bear in the house!

1 heavy-duty paper plate
Pencil
Black marker
Scissors

Black paper
Glue
Hole punch
18" of string

1. Place your paper plate so it's sitting right-side up, then take a pencil and outline the flat innermost circle of the paper plate. Next, you will draw the cheeks of the panda, 2 half-circles that meet at the nose in the center of the plate. First make a little dot in the approximate center of the plate to help guide your drawing. Starting on the left side of the inner circle you drew, a little lower than halfway up the plate, draw a half circle like a very shallow "u" that ends at the center dot. Do the same on the right side of the plate. Then draw a small, triangular nose in the middle of the plate, on top of the dot and the ends of the 2 cheek lines. Finally, draw the eyes: 2 large ovals with the bottoms slanting outward toward the bottom of the plate.

2. Go over all of the pencil lines with a black marker.

3. Use your scissors to cut off the rim of the paper plate. Then cut away the plate below the cheek lines as well.

4. Use scissors to cut small eye holes in the paper plate. They do not need to be perfect!

5. Out of black paper, cut 2 large ovals for eyes and a triangle for the nose that match up with the ovals and triangle you drew on the plate in Step 1. Then, use your paper plate eye holes as a template to cut eye holes in your black paper that match up with the eye holes you cut into the plate in Step 4.

6. For ears, cut 2 (1½") circles out of black paper and glue them to the back side of the paper mask right above the eye holes.

7. Glue the eyes and nose to the paper plate.

8. Hole-punch 1 hole on each side of the mask and tie 9" of string to each side. Use the string to tie the mask to your kid's face and let the panda roam free!

Tree Frog

If your kids are head over heels for frogs, they are going to be so excited about this Tree Frog craft. Hop with both feet into this project, and when the frog is complete have your kids play a game of leap frog with their friends!

1 thin paper plate
Paintbrush
Paint (I used green and red)
Scissors

2 sheets of colored paper (I used red and green)
Glue
Black marker

1. Fold your paper plate in half and paint the top side of the paper plate green. Allow the green paint to dry, and then paint the inside of the paper plate red. Then set the plate aside and allow to dry according to package instructions.

2. After the paper plate is completely dry, position it so the fold is at the top and cut 2 (1"-tall) semicircle-shaped flaps at the center near the top of the folded plate. These will be the frog's eyes.

3. Use your scissors to cut 2 (8"-long) checkmark-shaped legs out of your green paper. Then cut 2 (1" × 4") strips out of your green paper. Next, cut out 4 (4"-long) feet and 1 (8" × 1") tongue out of the red colored paper.

4. Use glue to attach the feet to the end of the legs and then glue each leg to the paper plate. The 2 checkmark-shaped legs should be attached directly behind the tree frog's eyes.

5. Use glue to attach the tongue to the center of the bottom of the frog's mouth. Then attach the 4"-long legs to the front of the paper plate on either side of the frog's tongue.

6. Use your black marker to add pupils to the frog's eyes, and give the frog an insect to eat, yum! I doodled a grasshopper onto green paper, roughly cut it out, and glued it to the end of the frog's tongue.

Awesome Fact

Did you know that the bright red eyes and bright colored feet of red-eyed tree frogs help the animal scare off predators?

Turtle Shaker

This craft doubles as a musical instrument—how fun is that? Have the older siblings make an extra turtle shaker for the little ones and keep everyone entertained. My 1-year-old thinks the turtle shaker is just about the greatest thing that ever existed, and I love that he loves it! Pair this craft with the other fun musical craft tutorials in this book—a Drum (see the project later in this chapter) and a Ribbon Wand (Chapter 4)—and put your dance pants on, because after this craft is made, it's time for a party!

Paintbrush
2 heavy-duty paper plates
Green paint

Cereal box
Scissors
Green washi tape
Stapler

½ cup dried beans
Black marker

1. Paint the top of one paper plate green, then allow the paint to dry according to package instructions.

2. While you are waiting for the paint to dry, disassemble your cereal box by gently ripping the seams on the side and the bottom of the box with your finger. Then, use scissors to cut 4 (3"-long) ovals out of a cereal box to use as the turtle's legs. Cut out a large 2" circle for a head and a small 1" triangle to use as a tail.

3. Once the paint is dry, decorate the turtle's shell with small square pieces of green washi tape.

4. Staple the turtle's head, legs, and tail to the inside of the green paper plate.

5. Fill the non-painted paper plate with ½ cup of beans, place the 2 paper plates together, and attach with a series of staples, placed approximately 2"–3" apart, until the plates are secure, to form the turtle.

6. Use the black marker to draw a face on the turtle's head and shake it to the music!

KEEP IT CREATIVE!

If you don't have beans on hand, any kind of pasta or rice will work too. If you only have a long pasta noodle, like spaghetti or linguine, just break up the noodles in a ziptop bag before using them. And if you don't have washi tape on hand you could also use green construction paper or green tissue paper, or even create a collage with green pages from a magazine!

Spider

While many adults find spiders creepy, young kids are intrigued by their 8 legs and speedy maneuvers. That's why this Spider craft is the perfect addition to Halloween décor, or a fun rainy day craft to complete while singing the itsy bitsy spider song, watching *Charlotte's Web*, or both!

Paintbrush
1 heavy-duty paper plate
Black paint
Scissors

10 sheets of colored paper (I used black)
Glue or stapler
White-out pen or white paint

1. Paint the backside of the paper plate black, and set it aside to dry according to package instructions.

2. Use scissors to cut out 8 (6" × 2") strips of black colored paper and 8 (2" × 3") rectangles of black colored paper. Then, snip off the ends of each of the 8 (2" × 3") rectangles at a 45-degree angle to give the rectangles points.

3. Attach 4 of the 6" × 2" strips to one side of the paper plate with glue—or, even easier, using a stapler. Then attach the other 4 (6" × 2") strips to the other side of the paper plate. Next glue 1 (2" × 3") piece to each 6" × 2" piece to form the spider's long legs.

Awesome Fact

Did you know that spiders are found on every continent of the world except Antarctica?

4. Draw a face on your spider with a white-out pen or white paint, and hang!

Ring Toss

This is a great craft for a group of kids to do together! Gather up a few kids and have them each decorate 3 rings. When they're done, send them outside to play ring toss. The winner gets to pick the next craft to make. Oh, and the thicker and sturdier the paper plates, the better the rings will fly!

3 heavy-duty paper plates
Pen or marker
Scissors
3 yards of yarn (optional)
Paint (I used pink) (optional)
Colored markers (optional)
1 (12") ruler

1. Place your paper plate so it's sitting right-side up, then take a pen or marker and outline the round, flat, center eating surface of the paper plate. Use your scissors to cut out this circle, being careful not to cut through the rim of the plate.

2. Decorate the rings with whatever you would like! I used yarn, paint, and markers to make each ring unique. If using yarn, first tie the yarn in a simple knot around the paper plate, leaving a long tail. Then wrap the paper plate in yarn and use the long string you left at the beginning of the plate to tie off at the end.

3. To set up the ring toss game, bury the ruler 2" deep in dirt, grass, or rocks and start tossing your rings! Whoever gets the most rings on the ruler, wins.

No-Mess Painting

This is my all-time favorite craft for the under-2 crowd. Creativity without the mess makes everyone happy! With this project, your little one is creatively occupied and you don't have to clean paint off clothes, couches, or body parts! It's a win-win!

1 (1-gallon) ziptop bag per piece of art
2–5 paint colors per ziptop bag (I used blue, green, pink, and white)
Duct tape
1 piece of 8" × 10" white paper per ziptop bag

1. Fill 1 (1-gallon) ziptop bag with 2–5 colors of paint.

2. Seal the zip at the top of the bag well, then tape the top and bottom of the ziptop bag to the table.

3. Place the plain white sheet of paper under the ziptop bag so that the colors are more vivid. Then, show your toddler how to blend the colors through the plastic or fingerpaint on top of the bag.

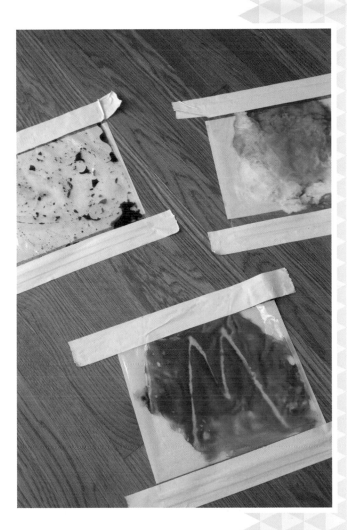

KEEP IT CREATIVE!

You can put anything in the ziptop bags! A few other ideas include baby oil and food coloring; shaving cream and food coloring; and oil, water, and food coloring. The possibilities are endless!

Paper Plate Necklace

Are your kids obsessed with jewelry and accessories? Well, let them fancy up any outfit with a paper plate statement necklace. Craft up a few of these necklaces and add them to the dress-up box to play with any day!

1 heavy-duty paper plate
Pen or marker
Scissors
Paintbrush
Paint (I used blue)

Pencil
Kitchen glass
Lid from 1 plastic milk jug
Black pen
Glue

1. Place your paper plate so it's sitting right-side up, then take a pen or marker and outline the flat innermost circle of the paper plate. Use your scissors to cut out the circle, being careful not to cut through the rim of the plate.

2. Paint the outer ring of the paper plate blue.

3. On the inside piece that you cut from the paper plate, use your pencil to trace 1 large circle using a glass from your kitchen.

4. Next, trace 4 smaller circles, using something small like the lid of a plastic milk jug. Decorate the large circle and the small circles any way you'd like. I used a black pen to create black and white patterns on my circles.

KEEP IT CREATIVE!

To make this necklace more masculine, consider adding a Spider-Man or Batman emblem to the large circle in the center. You can make it more feminine by changing up the colors or including pictures on the circles instead of simple designs.

5. Glue your 5 circles to the rim of the front of your paper plate, and then cut a slit in the back of the rim to allow the necklace to slide on and off of your neck.

Giraffe

Everybody loves giraffes, and these long-necked, orange, spotted creatures are always a hit with kids. Maybe it's because we don't get the opportunity to see them in person very often, but giraffes just seem so exotic! Take the kids on a virtual safari and teach them about the tallest mammal on Earth by making this standing giraffe with clothespin legs and fingerprint spots.

Pencil

2 pieces of construction paper
(I used yellow and orange)

Scissors

Orange marker

Black pen

Glue

2 clothespins

1. Use a pencil to draw the giraffe's body onto a piece of yellow construction paper. Start with a 3"-long horizontal rectangle, then add a 2"-long skinny neck, and a 1"-long oval for the head.

2. Use your scissors to cut the body of the giraffe out of the colored paper.

3. Color the pad of your pinky finger with orange marker and make pinky print spots on the giraffe's body. Allow the spots to dry for about 1 minute so that they do not smudge.

4. Use a black pen to outline the spots and add eyes and nose features.

5. Use scissors to cut a 1" orange rectangular-shaped tail. Then cut slits in the bottom third of the tail to mimic fringe-like hair texture. For the ears, first cut 2 small triangles out of yellow paper. The, cut 2 even smaller triangles out of orange paper. Glue the orange triangles inside of the yellow ones and glue to the top of the giraffe's head. Next, cut 2 (½"-long) orange lines to act as horns for the giraffe and attach them between his ears.

6. Attach the 2 clothespins to the giraffe to act as legs and make the giraffe stand tall anywhere you'd like!

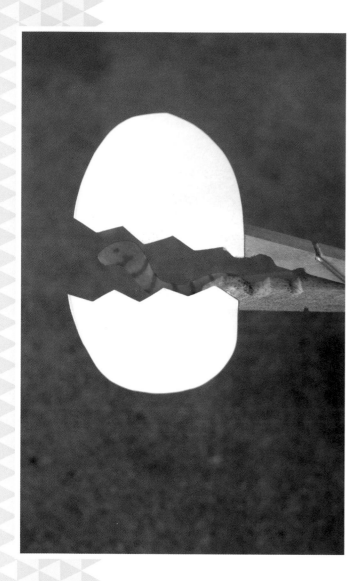

Egg Snakes

This is the perfect springtime craft when flowers are blooming and baby animals are born! Ask your kids how many animals they can think of that hatch from eggs. Then, use these instructions to craft up some of these super-fun, easy, Egg Snakes with clothespins, glue, scissors, and notecards.

Scissors
1 notecard
1 clothespin
Glue
Markers (I used light green and dark green)

1. Cut 1 (3"-long) oval out of a notecard, and then cut a zigzag line horizontally through the oval. This is the egg that your snake will be hatching out of.

2. With its zigzag edge facing upward, attach the bottom half of the egg to the front of the bottom half of the clothespin with a drop of glue. You'll want to attach the egg as close to the tip of the opening end of the clothespin as possible. Then, after making sure that the two halves line up nicely, attach the top half of the egg, zigzag side down, to the top half of the clothespin with a drop of glue.

3. Draw a small 1"-long snake on a notecard, color it in with markers, and cut it out.

4. Glue the snake to the back of the bottom half of the clothespin, making sure it is facing forward so that it will appear when you pinch the clothespin open!

Clothespin Art Display

This is a super-simple craft that allows kids to proudly display their notecard-sized art or printed photographs on any table, shelf, or counter in your home. Hopefully your refrigerator doesn't get jealous!

Washi tape
Clothespins
Scissors
Notecard-sized artwork or printed photographs

1. Unroll a roll of washi tape and place a clothespin on top of the sticky side of the tape. Use scissors to cut the tape at the end of the clothespin.

2. Push the tape down around the edges of the clothespin. If your washi tape is not wide enough, you might have to add another strip to the clothespin.

3. There are two different ways to attach the clothespins to photographs. To make a taller display, clip 1 clothespin vertically to each side of the bottom of the photo so that the photo is standing on "stilts." To make a shorter display, attach only 1 clothespin horizontally at the very bottom of the picture so that the clothespin acts as a base for the photo.

KEEP IT CREATIVE!

If you don't have washi tape on hand, try permanent markers or paint pens to make designs, patterns, or even write words directly onto the clothespins.

Brown Bag Placemats

Hosting a dinner party? Thanksgiving? Taco Tuesday? Get the kids on this craft, pronto! Brown bag placemats are a fun and easy way to quickly spruce up and personalize any table setting. Plus the kids will love that they get to be part of the process. Enjoy!

Scissors
1 brown paper bag (per 2 placemats)
Pencil
Dinner plate
Permanent markers

1. Cut open the seams of a brown paper bag so that it lies flat. Cut off the bottom rectangular piece of the brown bag and, if there are handles, cut them off.

2. Cut the brown bag into large squares, with the size determined by the size of your dinner plates and brown bags. The bigger you make the squares, the more room you will have for decorating!

3. Crumple your brown bag squares, but be careful not to rip them.

4. Smooth out the brown bag squares, and then use a pencil to trace around a dinner plate in the center of each square.

5. Grab a permanent marker and trace over your circle. Add doodles around the circle to emphasize where the plate goes. Get creative! You can add flowers, stripes, polka dots, or even personalize the place mat with the names of the people who will be at the table.

Faux Leather Painting

My husband, Andy, learned how to make faux leather paintings from paper bags in 3rd grade. He claims this is the only craft he ever enjoyed making when he was a little boy. I figure there must be other parents who have little ones who don't like to craft, and maybe, just maybe, faux leather painting will inspire a creative spark for your child as it did for Andy! I also really like this craft because you get two art pieces for the price of one. The wax paper creates a mirror image after ironing and you can hang it in your window as a sun catcher!

Scissors
1 brown paper bag
Pencil
Crayons

Wax paper
Iron
Dish Towel

1. Cut open the seams of a brown paper bag so that it lies flat. Cut off the bottom rectangular piece of the brown bag and, if there are handles, cut them off.

2. Cut a large 8" × 12" rectangle from the brown bag.

3. Use a pencil to draw a picture, and then use crayons to color over the picture. Make sure the wax from the crayons goes onto the bag very dark and thick.

4. Crumple up your art work! Don't worry if the edges rip a little—you want it to look old and tattered.

5. Cut a piece of wax paper that covers your crayon drawing.

6. Heat up the iron and sandwich the crayon drawing between the ironing board and the wax paper. Make sure the waxy side of the wax paper is in contact with the side of the paper bag that has the drawing on it. Lay a thin dishtowel or rag over the top of the wax paper to protect your iron and iron over the entire piece for 30–60 seconds, or until the dishrag is hot to the touch. After ironing, carefully remove the dishtowel and wax paper to reveal your faux painted leather.

7. Don't discard the wax paper though; trim the sides and hang it in a window as a sun catcher!

Brown Bag Gift Wrap

After the kids make this cute, free gift wrap, you'll never use store-bought gift wrap again. Seriously! It's that fun and easy, and it instantly personalizes any gift. Plus, think about having your kids wrap all of their own friends' birthday gifts and even helping out with holiday wrapping? How great does that sound? You can thank me later!

Scissors
1 brown paper bag
Tape
Permanent markers

1. Cut open the seams of a brown paper bag so that it lies flat. Cut off the bottom rectangular piece of the brown bag and, if there are handles, cut them off. The goal is to make the brown bag lie open flat.

2. Crumple the brown bag. And then crumple it some more!

3. Next, smooth out the paper bag and wrap the gift box as usual with the brown bag, taping down the sides with tape.

4. Use permanent markers to decorate the front of the wrapping paper. Doodle names, gift tags, bows, rocket ships, words, or encouraging phrases . . . heck, you can even doodle some donuts if you'd like!

KEEP IT CREATIVE!

Before you get too far into this project, make sure that you have enough brown paper to wrap your box. A typical grocery bag will wrap a shirt box. Also, when wrapping your box, know that packing tape works a lot better to ensure that the thick grocery bag stays stuck, but you can use whatever tape you have on hand!

Western Vest

Thanks to brown paper bags, dress-up just got better—and less expensive! Just add boots and a red bandana to this brown bag Western Vest, and you've got yourself the perfect cowgirl/cowboy outfit. And once you get the brown bag cut into a vest, you can decorate it to be a variety of costumes—construction worker, police officer, or firefighter, to name a few. The ideas are endless!

Scissors
1 brown paper bag
Measuring tape
Markers
Cereal box
Aluminum foil
Tape or glue

1. Cut open the seams of a brown paper bag so that it lies flat. Cut off the bottom rectangular piece of the brown bag. If there are handles, cut them off.

2. Turn the bag so that the plain brown paper faces down.

3. Measure the width of the child's back and add 2". This is how long you will want the back of the vest to be. For my 1-year-old, I made the vest 11" wide.

4. Fold and cut the vest so that the back is the desired length and the front of the vest opens in the center.

5. Cut a "V" for the neckline.

6. Cut 2 circles in the folds for arm holes, then crumple the brown bag to make it look more worn and leathery. Next, smooth out the vest so that it lies flat.

7. Cut a 2" strip of fringe around the bottom of the vest.

8. Decorate the front of the vest with markers.

9. Disassemble your cereal box by gently ripping the seams on the side and bottom of the box with your finger. Then, cut a 5" star out of the cereal box and cover it with tin foil. Then attach it to the vest with tape or glue.

Brown Bag Pencil Holder

Organization is an important skill to teach kids, and this adorable Pencil Holder is guaranteed to keep writing utensils neat and tidy. Not to mention that the little ones will love how simple and easy this craft is to make! Just for fun, ask the kids what other creatures might live in a knothole in a tree. I added an owl, but there are many other options.

Ruler
1 tin can
Scissors
1 brown paper bag
Brown marker
Glue
Black marker
2 pieces of colored paper (I used yellow and orange)
Hole punch

1. Use a ruler to measure the height of your tin can, then cut a long rectangular strip of brown paper bag that is long enough to fit around the can and 1" taller than the can (so it can be folded over the top of the can to hide the rim).

2. Crumple up your rectangular piece of brown paper bag.

3. Smooth out the brown rectangle, then lay it flat and use a brown marker to draw vertical lines and swirls all over the paper. The goal is to make the brown bag mimic tree bark.

4. Wrap the brown paper bag around the tin can and use glue to adhere the bag to the tin can.

5. With a black marker, draw a large 2" oval in the middle of the tin can. This will be the hole in the tree where the owl will sit.

6. Make a tiny owl out of a scrap of brown paper bag. The owl's body should be about a 1" brown oval with 2 tiny triangles on top for ears. Then use your hole punch to punch out 2 circles from the yellow colored paper to form the owl's eyes. Next, cut a small triangle from the orange colored paper to form the owl's beak. Use glue to attach the eyes and beak to the paper bag owl, then use the black marker to draw ears, pupils, and wings.

7. Finally, glue the owl into the tree hole.

KEEP IT CREATIVE!

If you think glue might get too messy for this project, feel free to use double-sided sticky tape or Elmer's CraftBond Glue Spots. Glue spots are typically used in paper crafting. They are clear, adhesive spots that are easy to apply and are mess free!

Drum

This Drum will be the perfect addition to your family band! This project is also a great use for those giant popcorn tins you get during the holidays. If you did not save one this year, don't worry! Any tin can with a lid will work, including baby formula, coffee, or cookie tins.

Ruler
Any size tin can with a lid
Scissors
1 brown paper bag
Black marker
Hole punch

1 sheet of colored paper (I used orange)
Glue
2 yards of string
Tape
Paint stir sticks

1. Use a ruler to measure the height of your can, then cut a long rectangular strip of brown paper bag that is long enough to fit around the can and 1" taller than the can (so it can be folded over the top of the can to hide the rim).

2. Crumple up your rectangular piece of brown paper bag.

3. Once your brown bag is nice and crumpled, it is time to decorate your drum. Remember, there is no right or wrong way to do this part! Lay your rectangle flat, and use a ruler and a black marker to make diagonal intersecting lines all over the brown paper bag. I glued orange punched-out holes where the black diagonal lines intersect, then I wrapped green yarn around the drum to add a little more texture and secured the ends of the yarn with small pieces of tape.

4. Now attach the brown paper bag to the tin can. Tape one end of the brown bag to the can, then wrap the brown bag around the can and use glue to adhere the bag to itself.

5. Put the lid back on the tin, give your kid some paint stir sticks to use as drumsticks, and your drum is ready for its first performance!

KEEP IT CREATIVE!

You can use a lot of different things as drumsticks, including chopsticks, kitchen utensils, Popsicle sticks, or twigs—or even just your hands!

Egg Carton Camel

This fun craft turns an everyday egg carton into a camel with just 3 simple craft supplies! If you know the silly song about Sally the camel, consider crafting a camel with 5 humps, just for fun!

Scissors
Egg carton
Paintbrush
Brown paint
4 clothespins
Black pen

1. Using scissors, cut out 2 egg holders from an egg carton. These will be the camel's humps, so make sure to keep the egg holders attached to each other.

2. Cut out the camel's head and tail from the lid of the egg carton. The camel's head should be shaped like a backward letter "Z," and be about 2½" long. The tail should be about 1" long and shaped like a simple check mark with fringe cut ¾ of the way up.

3. Paint all of the camel parts brown and let them dry completely.

4. To assemble, cut slits in the front and back of the egg holders (camel's humps) to hold the head and tail. The slits should be cut in the middle of the egg holders so that the head and tail do not fall out of the bottom of the egg carton. Then just slide the camel's head into the front slit and the camel's tail into the back slit.

5. Attach the 4 clothespins, 2 on each side of each egg holder, to make the legs.

6. Use a black pen to draw the camel's eyes, mouth, and a little mark to define the ear.

Awesome Fact

Did you know that camels can drink up to 30 gallons of water in just 13 minutes?

Egg Carton Flowers

These flowers are pretty and fun to make—and they never die! Best of all, the kids will enjoy making their own unique bouquets out of egg cartons and will love seeing them on display, in their own bedroom or maybe even in their teacher's classroom. Think about attaching a handwritten note that says "Thanks for helping me bloom this year!" and brighten any teacher's day!

Scissors
Egg carton
Paintbrush
Paint (I used blue, orange, pink, and green)
Wooden Skewers (1 per flower)
Tape
1 sheet of colored paper (I used yellow)
Glue

1. Cut the egg carton into 1-egg sections, and then use scissors to form multiple petals, make fringe, or cut pointy petals.

2. Paint the inside and outside of each 1-egg section in the color of your choosing. You could also paint the petals alternating colors or even random colors. After painting, set the flowers aside and allow to dry according to package instructions.

4. Cut 1 (1") circle of yellow colored paper per flower, and use glue to adhere it to the center of the flower, covering up the top of the skewer.

5. Next, add leaves to your flowers! Just cut a few leaf shapes from the leftover egg carton, paint them green, and stick them onto your skewer under the flower. Use the skewer to poke a hole in the leaf and slide the leaf onto the skewer under the flower.

3. To assemble your flowers, poke a small hole with the pointy end of the skewer in one side of the egg carton flower near the bottom of the egg indent, then insert the skewer. Allow about ½" of the skewer to stick through. Tape the skewer to the bottom of the egg carton.

Earth

The Earth coffee filter craft is also a great way to introduce little ones to the idea of continents and oceans. In order to show the kids all 7 continents, you can make 2 coffee filter Earth crafts for double the fun!

1 coffee filter
Colored markers (I used blue and green)
Pie dish

Paintbrush
Cup of water
1 brown paper bag
Black pen

1. Roughly draw the continents on the coffee filter with green marker and fill them in with green swirls and stripes. Use a blue marker to fill in the oceans with doodles and designs. It is okay to have a little bit of white showing, but you want the majority of the filter covered in marker.

2. Lay the coffee filter in a pie dish. Then, dip a paintbrush in a cup of water and paint the water onto your coffee filter. Watch the colors swirl together.

Awesome Fact

Here's a trick for remembering the order of the planets in our solar system, starting closet to the sun. Ready? My Very Energetic Mom Just Served Us Noodles. The first letter of each word represents the first letter of a planet: M=Mercury, V=Venus, E=Earth, M=Mars, J=Jupiter, S=Saturn, U=Uranus, N=Neptune.

3. Let the coffee filter dry on the brown paper bag. If you lay it in the sun to dry, this should only take a few hours. If it stays inside, you should let it dry overnight.

4. Use a black pen to roughly outline the continents and oceans.

Leaves

In Texas, we don't exactly have four seasons, so to get my fall fix in I like to craft up my own beautifully colored leaves. I know your kids will *fall* in love with this coffee filter leaf craft too! Before you and the kids start this craft, take a little stroll outside and gather up a few leaves. Examine their shapes and color to use as inspiration to make your own.

Coffee filters (1 per 4–5 leaves)
Colored markers (I used red, blue, orange, green, and brown)
Paintbrush
Cup of water
1 heavy-duty paper plate
Scissors
Tape

1. Cover the coffee filter with red, blue, orange, and green marker designs. Be sure to leave a little white showing on the coffee filter so that the colors don't blend into a brown blob.

2. Place the coffee filter on the plate. Dip a paintbrush in water and paint on your coffee filter. Watch the colors swirl together.

3. Let the coffee filter dry on a heavy-duty paper plate.

4. Use a brown marker to draw leaf shapes onto the coffee filter. You should be able to fit 4–5 leaves on 1 coffee filter.

5. Use scissors to cut the leaf shapes out of the coffee filter.

6. Tape the leaves to a window and let the light shine through!

Peacock

As children, my five siblings and I were lucky to have a nearby park with a playground and peacocks! We loved playing among the peacocks and waiting (not so patiently) to see the male peacocks fan their tail feathers. Your kids will love watching the colors swirl together on the peacock's tail in this coffee filter craft!

1 coffee filter
Colored markers (I used blue, green, and orange)
1 heavy-duty paper plate
Paintbrush
Cup of water

Scissors
5 sheets of colored paper (I used 1 sheet each of black, white, yellow, green, and blue)
Hole punch
Glue
Toothpick
Black pen

1. Cover the coffee filter with blue, green, and orange marker designs.

2. Lay the coffee filter on a heavy-duty paper plate. Then dip a paintbrush in water and paint the water onto your coffee filter. Watch the colors swirl together.

3. Let the coffee filter dry on the paper plate.

4. To make the peacock's head, cut a spoon shape out of black construction paper that is almost as tall as your coffee filter folded in half.

5. Use a hole punch to make 2 white eyes, then cut out a 1½"-long yellow triangle for the beak. Glue the eyes and the beak to the head. For the Peacock's crest, cut thin strips of green and blue construction paper and wrap each one around a toothpick to give it curl. Glue these to the back of the peacock's head.

6. Fold your coffee filter in half and use glue to secure. Then use a black pen to draw feathers and swirls on your coffee filter.

7. Glue the head to the coffee filter and enjoy your Peacock!

Awesome Fact

We know this beautiful bird as a peacock, but this is actually only the correct name for the male. Females are known as peahens, and babies are known as peachicks. Collectively, they are known as peafowl!

Cereal Box Pineapple Puzzle

This is a craft that can be made and enjoyed by your kids for years to come! But it's not just your kids who will love this cereal box puzzle. They are also a fun craft to mail as gifts to friends and family. If sending as a gift, think about adding a personalized message for the recipient to find after he finishes the puzzle!

Cereal box
Scissors
Pencil
Paintbrush
Paint (I used yellow and green)
Permanent marker
Ruler

1. Disassemble your cereal box by gently ripping the seams on the side and bottom of the box with your finger.

2. Cut one side of the cereal box off with your scissors so that you have a large rectangle.

3. Use your pencil to draw a 7–8"-tall oval. This will be the fruit of the pineapple. Then use your pencil to draw spikey leaves coming out of the top of the pineapple. The spikey leaves should start at the top of the oval and reach the top of the rectangle.

4. Use a paintbrush to paint the round oval yellow and the spikey pineapple leaves green. Wait for the paint to dry according to package instructions.

5. Add details to the pineapple with a permanent marker. I added black arrows to the yellow part of the pineapple and outlined the entire picture with a black marker.

6. Now, use a ruler to add diagonal lines to the background of the pineapple. This will make putting the puzzle together a little easier.

7. Turn your picture over, and use a pencil to draw interlocking puzzle piece lines. Cut out the puzzle pieces with your scissors.

8. Put your puzzle together and take it apart over and over again! Or even better, send it to a friend in the mail!

KEEP IT CREATIVE!

Encourage your kids to be creative and draw whatever they want on the cereal box. A scene at the beach, a portrait of their dog, or a lizard are fun options! If sending this as a gift in the mail, draw something that represents the gift recipient to make it even a little more special.

Cereal Box Gift Bag

You already learned how to make gift wrap out of brown paper bags earlier in this chapter, but here's another option for wrapping oddly shaped gifts. Kids can do this one all on their own just by turning a cereal box inside out and getting creative! I decorated the front of the gift box with a simple black permanent marker, but feel free to use paint, tissue paper, or construction paper, or create a collage from a magazine.

Cereal box
Permanent marker
Tape
Hole punch
Notecard (optional)
Glass (optional)
Pen or pencil (optional)
Scissors
20" of ribbon

1. Disassemble your cereal box by gently ripping the seams on the side and bottom of the box with your finger.

2. Turn the cereal box so that the outside of the box is face down, and use the permanent marker to draw triangles on the blank side of the box.

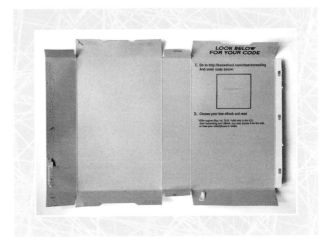

3. Fold the box so that you reconstruct it inside out and the design that you just drew is on the outside of the box. Use tape to secure your new box.

4. Use a hole punch to punch 2 holes in the top of both long sides of the box. The holes should be about 4" apart from one another. These will hold the ribbon handles of the finished gift box.

5. If you want to, use a notecard to make a gift tag. Grab a glass from the kitchen and trace a circle, then cut it out. Punch a hole in the top of the circle.

6. Cut a piece of ribbon that is 10" long. Pull it through one hole at the top of the bag, tie a knot on the end inside the bag to keep it from pulling back out through the hole, and then pull the other end of the ribbon through the hole on the same side of the box and knot it at the end. Repeat this process with another 10" piece of ribbon on the other side of the box. If you made a gift card, string the tag through one side of the handle before passing it through the punched hole and knotting it.

Snowman Tin Can

The snowman tin can comes from the creative genius of Kelly Rowe of *http://livelaughrowe.com*. This little tin can snowman will cure everyone's winter blues in no time! And I love that the kids will not only enjoy crafting Frosty the (tin can) Snowman, but possibly even pass on their crafty treat as a little treat to friends, neighbors, and teachers for the holidays. Spread the winter cheer everywhere! (Oh, and if your kids are *Frozen* fans, Frosty was just renamed Olaf!)

Soup can (or any can in the shape and size of your choice)
Acrylic paint (Kelly used white, black, and orange)
Paintbrush
3 toothpicks

1. Clean and remove the label from the can, then gather your supplies.

2. Using acrylic paint, paint the entire outside of the can white and set aside to dry according to package instructions.

3. Once your can is dry, use black and orange paint to paint on a simple snowman face. For the snowman's eyes and mouth, use a toothpick and black paint to make simple black "coal" dots. The "carrot" nose is just one very large orange triangle with rounded corners!

KEEP IT CREATIVE!

If you don't have acrylic paint on hand, consider wrapping your tin can in a plain white piece of paper instead!

Layered Straw Necklace

This layered straw necklace is not only fun and easy to make, it also adds a nice pop of color to any plain T-shirt! Kids will love sorting and stringing the straw beads, and you'll love that this craft is enhancing your kids' fine motor skills.

Scissors
6 different colored plastic straws
Muffin tin
24" of string

KEEP IT CREATIVE!

It honestly is not that important how many beads you string on each layer or which bead you pull the string back through. The straw necklace is supposed to be layered and fun! If you don't like your final product, just unstring it and try again.

1. Cut the straws into small beadlike segments. The straw beads can be anywhere from ¼" long to 1" long. You'll need about 40 beads to make one necklace. It's fun to have a variety of lengths and colors to choose from.

2. Separate the colored straw beads into a muffin tin for easy access.

3. Cut 1 (24") piece of string per necklace.

4. String 13 straw beads onto your string. I choose to do a random color order, but a pattern would be fun too.

5. String 10 more straw beads onto the string and then pull the string through the first bead you placed on the string. Now, both pieces of string will be on the same side.

6. String 8 more beads on and then pull the string through the first bead from your second row.

7. String 7-8 more beads onto the string and pull the string through the first bead you placed on the string. Now, both pieces of string will be on the same side again.

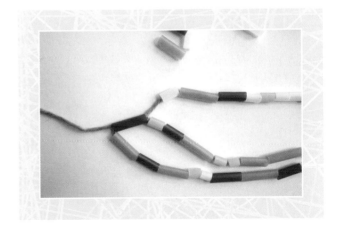

8. Now to make the last strand on your necklace, string 6-/ more beads onto your string. Then tie the 2 ends of the string together and wear with pride!

I Spy Jar

I spy with my little eye an easy craft to make and a great game to play with kids! Don't forget to pack this one in the car for a day full of errand running or even a long road trip. The kids will love searching for small items like a small green dog or a tiny pink donut in the car, on airplanes, or even just hanging out at home. This is one of those crafts that keeps on giving!

Mason jar
8–15 small trinkets (paper clip, jewelry, stickers, charms, buttons, game pieces, painted pebbles, thumb tack, etc.)
Funnel or piece of paper
Rice
Paint (I used blue)
Paintbrush
Pen or pencil
1 notecard
Scissors
Thin marker
Clear packing tape

8. Sandwich the metal circle, notecard circle, and Mason jar ring together and screw onto your jar. This game can be played alone or with a friend. If playing alone, start with the first item on the list and shake and move the jar until you spy all of the items.

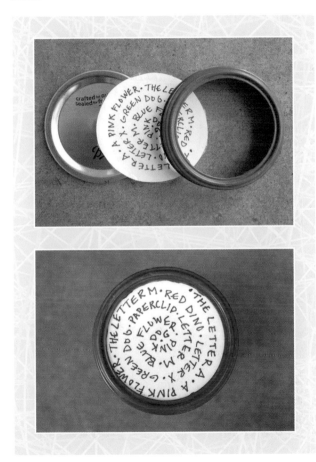

1. Depending on the size of your Mason jar, place 3–5 small trinkets in the bottom of your clean jar.

2. Use a funnel or fold a piece of paper into a cone shape and pour rice inside to fill your jar halfway.

3. Add 3–5 more small trinkets and fill the jar to 2" below the rim.

4. Add 3–5 more small trinkets, then fill the jar with rice until there is only 1" of empty space at the top.

5. Using blue paint, paint the ring that goes around the Mason jar when it is closed. Allow this to dry according to package instructions.

6. Trace the inside of the Mason jar rim onto a notecard. Use your scissors to cut out the circle notecard shape.

7. On the notecard circle using a thin marker, write down all of the items inside of your I Spy Jar, and then cover the circle in clear packing tape.

Cork Necklace

The Cork Necklace is the result of the creative genius of Amy Johnson at *www.makermama.com*. I love that this necklace is so chic it could be given to Grandma, a baby-sitter, or a teacher as a gift made by the kids! And if you don't want to use the pink and gold paint shown in the pictures, feel free to use whatever colors you like. Think about adding polka dots, stripes, or even words to the corks. This is where you can let your creativity flow!

Corkscrew
3 corks
Paintbrush
Paint (Amy used pink and gold)
18" of single strand embroidery thread
1 (2") or longer doll needle

1. Use a corkscrew to pierce through the center of the 3 corks. Depending on the age and ability of your kid, this step could be done by an adult or with adult supervision.

2. Paint 2 corks with a layer of pink paint and 1 cork with a layer of gold paint, then set aside to dry according to package instructions. Once the corks are dry, add another layer of paint to each cork and set aside to dry.

3. Thread your embroidery thread onto a sewing needle, then put the needle through each of the corks.

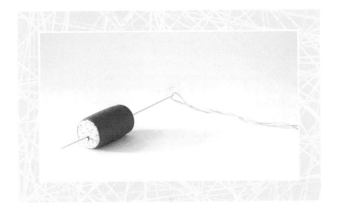

4. Tie the 2 ends of the embroidery thread together, so that the necklace can slip on and off of your head easily.

Water Bottle Beaver

If you have a child who loves to build, he's going to be very impressed by the building that a beaver can do! This super-easy project is made out of a water bottle, plastic bag, and some colored paper. And it's so easy that your kids will probably ask to build more than just one!

Empty (12-ounce) plastic water bottle, dry, with label removed
2 or 3 brown plastic bags from the grocery store
Cereal box
Pencil
Kitchen glass
Scissors
1 sheet of paper (I used white)
Black marker
Glue
Tape

1. Fill the clean, dry water bottle with 2 or 3 brown plastic bags.

2. Disassemble your cereal box by gently ripping the seams on the side and bottom of the box with your finger. With a pencil, use a kitchen glass to trace a 4–5" wide circle onto a cereal box. Then, use the bottle cap from the water bottle to trace semi-circles on the top sides of the circle. These will be the beaver's ears. Use scissors to cut out the entire piece. This will be the beaver's head.

3. Use a pencil to draw a 6"-long, 3"-wide rounded check mark shape on the cereal box. Use scissors to cut this out. This will be the beaver's tail.

4. Use the water bottle cap again to trace 2 (1") circles on white paper, then use scissors to cut them out of the white sheet of paper. These will be eyes. Next, use a pencil to draw 2 (1"-long) rectangles on a piece of white paper, then use scissors to cut then out. These will be used as teeth.

5. Use a black marker to add details to the beaver's face. First add a wide, curved "W" shape to the bottom third of the beaver's head and add a triangular-shaped nose to the peak in the middle of the "W." Then add 2 tiny black semi circles, about the size of your pinky nail, to the ears and a zigzag line in between the ears to represent fur. Next, add 2 black pupils to the white circles.

6. Use glue to attach the circles to the top half of the beaver's head. Then glue the teeth just underneath the "W" shape you drew earlier.

7. To finish the beaver, add crisscross lines to the tail and tape the tail to the bottom, back of the water bottle with the crisscross lines facing the front of the bottle. Then tape the beaver's head to the top of the water bottle. And now your beaver is ready to build dams!

Awesome Fact

The largest dam built by beavers is in Wood Buffalo National Park in Canada, spans 2,800 feet (about 9 football fields!), and can be seen from space.

Chapter 3

OFFICE

Whether your office gets an entire room in your house or just an itty bitty nook in the living room, I am almost positive that you will have all of the office supplies needed to make the kids' crafts found in this chapter. The office chapter is inspired by everyday office supplies, including permanent markers (Sharpies are my favorite!), single-hole punch, magazines, and tape. We will even be diving into your paper shredder to craft up a sheep. Your kids are going to love the Tie-Dye Shoelaces, Faux Stained Glass, Thumbtack Ghost Pumpkins, Matching Game, and more! So get into your office and start tracking down the materials for these super-fun crafts.

Race Track

Did you know that you can build a race track almost anywhere? It's true. All you need is tape and a hard surface. Cement, carpet, or hardwood floors all work perfectly. And don't be afraid to get the furniture involved, either! Race tracks love to go up couches, down chairs, and across tables! And one of the nice things about masking tape, in particular, is that it will easily peel off of almost every surface. If you are unsure, do a tiny tape test before taping down an entire track.

Pencil
Paper
Tape (masking tape, washi tape, and electrical tape work best)
Scissors
Chalk (optional)
Toy cars

1. Draw a simple plan on a scrap piece of paper. Do you want pit stops? Parking lots? How wide does your race track need to be? Do you want short cuts? Adding and subtracting track is super simple, so don't let the kids stress about the rough draft too much.

2. Copy the design drawn on paper using the tape on the ground. Start by unrolling the tape and cutting 1 long strip the desired length of the race track section you are building. Continue taping down pieces of track until you are happy with the shape.

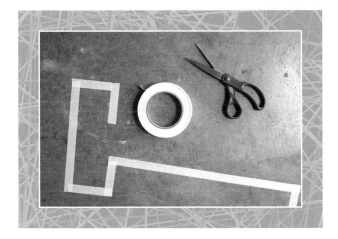

3. Once the outline of the race track is completed, either use small pieces of masking tape to make road lines inside of the track or, if the race track is outside, use chalk!

4. Give the toy cars to your kids and let them have fun!

KEEP IT CREATIVE!

If you'd like, you can add all kinds of things to your race track. For instance, small rocks make great road blocks or jumps. Want trees? You can make some out of books in a project later in this chapter. And I've heard that toilet paper roll animals from Chapter 4 make a great audience for a car race!

Monogram

This is a quick, fun craft for kids of any age—and it utilizes two of my very favorite craft materials: a cereal box and tape! Kids will love that they can personalize this really awesome piece of wall art and hang it above their bed or on their bedroom door to give their space some personality!

Cereal box
Scissors
Pencil
Washi tape

1. Disassemble your cereal box by gently ripping the seams on the side and bottom of the box with your finger.

2. Cut off one side of the cereal box with your scissors so that you have a large rectangle. Typically this is about 8½" × 11".

3. Use a pencil and draw 1 block letter that fills the space.

4. Cut out your letter with scissors.

5. Use different kinds of tape to decorate your monogram. Make patterns or use random stripes of tape! Also consider using white scotch tape and markers to make the plain white tape come alive! Don't be afraid to leave stripes of the raw cardboard. That can be really pretty too!

KEEP IT CREATIVE!

If you are uncomfortable free-handing block letters, you can make a stencil on your computer using Microsoft Word. Use a font of your choice and enlarge the font to fill your space! Then print out the letter, cut it out, and trace it onto your cereal box for a perfect letter.

Tin Can Vase

The kids will adore taking a nature walk, picking flowers and greenery, and then making a vase to hold all of their treasures! All you need to do is put tape around a tin can and you have a great looking vase that shows off your kid's personality—and adds a little color and pizzazz to the kitchen table!

Tin can with label removed
Tape (I used duct tape, electrical tape, washi tape, masking tape, etc.)
Scissors
Permanent marker (I used black)

1. Clean out a tin can and let it dry completely. Wrap the tape roll around the outside of the can at the very top, making sure to leave 1" hanging over the top of the rim. Use scissors to cut the tape from the roll and use your fingers to ensure that the tape sticks to the tin can.

2. Use scissors to cut slits every 1" along the tape that is sticking up over the rim. Then, carefully fold the tape over the top of the can. I like to cover the rim of the can because it is sharp and you don't want kids (or adults) cutting their fingers on it!

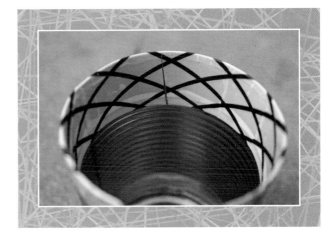

3. Continue wrapping the tape around the can until the entire can is covered.

4. Use different kinds of tape to decorate the outside of the can simply by taping strips around the tin can.

5. Use permanent markers to doodle shapes, words, or designs onto the solid colored pieces of tape. Get creative!

Superhero Mask

Turn any kid into a superkid with this handy-dandy, super-easy-to-make duct tape Superhero Mask. The best part about this project is that you can make the superhero mask in any shape, size, or color to fit any kid in your household! Kids also love that the mask actually feels good on their face since the tape is smooth and flat.

Scissors
Duct tape
White paper
Pencil

Black marker
Hole punch
String (or ribbon or elastic)

1. Cut 1 piece of duct tape that is 10" long. Place the piece of tape on the table or ground, sticky-side up, and use 2 rocks to hold the edges of the tape down if needed.

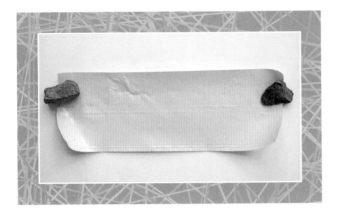

2. Cut another 10"-long piece of tape and place it about ½" overlapping on the bottom of the first piece of tape so that you now have 1 large duct tape rectangle.

3. Cut 2 more pieces of 10" tape and place directly over the first 2 pieces, so that the sticky parts of the tape are stuck together.

4. Now make the mask template. Grab a white piece of paper and draw a simple mask shape with a pencil. Fold the mask template in half at the center to make sure that your mask shape is symmetrical. If not, use your pencil to make it symmetrical. Once you're happy with the shape, use your scissors to cut out your mask template.

5. Use your template to trace the mask shape onto your duct tape rectangle with a black marker.

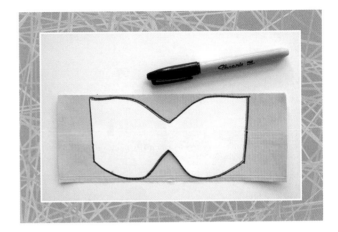

6. Cut the mask out of the duct tape rectangle with scissors. Then use the marker to draw 1 oval eye hole. Cut out the eye hole using scissors.

7. Fold the mask in half and trace the eye hole you just cut onto the second half of the mask with the black marker. Cut out the second eye hole with a pair of scissors.

8. Punch a hole in each side of the mask and attach a piece of string, ribbon, or elastic to each side, making sure the two ties are long enough to comfortably tie the mask on. Then, let the superhero games begin!

Feather Key Chain

Kids will love adding funky Feather Key Chains to every zipper pull in sight! Backpacks will get spruced up in no time with rainbow-colored feathers of all sizes. You can also consider making duct tape feathers into necklaces or earrings too!

Duct Tape Feathers
Scissors
Duct tape

Key Chain
Hole punch
Key ring

1. **For Duct Tape Feathers:** To make a 3" feather, cut 2 (3") pieces of duct tape.

2. Carefully stick the 2 pieces of tape together, sticky side to sticky side. This can be hard to get right, so be patient!

3. Cut a simple feather shape out of your tape. The feather should be pointy at one end and have a flat base at the other end. Then, cut fringe on both sides of your feather, being careful not to cut the slits up too high. This is especially important when making small feathers, since you do not want the slits to touch the hole that you will be punching at the top. Each slit should be about ½" long, but it totally depends on the width of the feather you made!

4. **For Key Chain:** Use a hole punch to punch a single hole in the top of the feather and then slip the feathers onto a key ring.

Candy Wrapper Bow Barrettes

These little treasures were actually one of my favorite crafts to make as a kid. I mean, I had to eat a bag of candy so that I could craft. Sold! I recently learned that the candy wrapper bows were a craft brought to our house by my Aunt Maria Elena. When I was a child, my mom, sister, and I spent many hours crafting up hundreds of candy bag bows for us and to share with our friends. I know you and the kids will enjoy this craft just as much as my family did!

3 candy wrappers in 3 different sizes (I used a jelly
  bean bag wrapper, a Skittles bag wrapper, and a Laffy
  Taffy wrapper)
Clear packing tape
Scissors (pinking shears or regular scissors)
15" of ribbon
Hair clips
Hot-glue gun (optional)

1. You can use almost any candy wrapper to make bows—just be careful when opening the package. Ideally, you want to open the wrapper cleanly at the seam on the side of the package.

2. Remove (and eat, toss, or save) all of the candy. I suggest eat! Next, sandwich the candy wrapper between 2 pieces of clear packing tape.

3. Cut the candy wrapper out of the clear packing tape with pinking shears or regular scissors so that you have a "laminated" candy wrapper.

4. Use 10" of ribbon to cinch up the center of the wrapper and tie a knot. Then, if desired, use the rest of the ribbon to form a pretty bow on the top of your candy wrapper, cutting off any excess until the ends of the bow have reached the desired length.

5. There are 2 choices for attaching the hair clip. 1: Use a hot-glue gun and put a line of glue on the bottom side of the bow. Then place the hair clip into the glue and set aside to dry according to package instructions. 2: Slip the hair clip right under the knot you tied the bow with. The second option works well if you are using a very thin ribbon.

Pencil Bag

Tanner Bell and Courtney Chambers are a teen crafting duo who run the website A Little Craft In Your Day (*www.alittlecraftinyourday.com*). Courtney admits that she has a sweet tooth. More specifically, she declares, "I love candy with all of my heart!" And instead of throwing the wrappers away, she likes to use them to make functional, beautiful pencil bags. The best part is that no sewing is involved!

2 (14-ounce) candy bags
Scissors
Clear packing tape
1 (7") zipper
Duct tape

1. Carefully open your 14-ounce bag of candy so that you do not rip the front of the package.

2. Cut the front of the candy wrappers off so that you have 2 rectangles.

3. Line the rectangles up, short end to short end, with both wrappers facing upward. Then cover both wrappers with clear packing tape, creating 1 very long candy wrapper rectangle.

4. All zippers typically have about ½" of fabric that surrounds them, which is usually what is used to sew a zipper onto fabric. This is an easy kid craft and we don't sew, so we are going to use clear packing tape to attach the zipper! It will go at the top of the right half of the candy wrapper rectangle. With the zipper zipped up, align it at the top of the wrapper with the zipper pull on the right side and tape it in place with clear packing tape, folding the excess tape over the top of the wrapper.

5. Flip the rectangle over and cover the entire back side with duct tape.

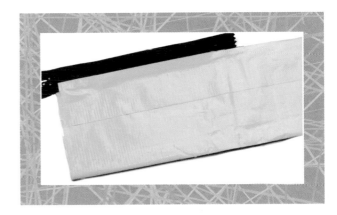

6. Fold your candy wrapper rectangle in half, over the tape seam, so that you have the front sides of both candy wrappers facing each other. When the zipper is unzipped, there are 2 sides to the zipper. The first side is already attached; now we are going to attach the other side of the zipper with clear packing tape. Use clear packing tape to secure the side and bottom of the zipper pouch. Fill with goodies, and carry around with pride!

Dream Catcher

Dream catchers are a Native American tradition, and are believed to "catch" your dreams. The good dreams are allowed to pass through, while the bad dreams get caught in the web. Cure bad dreams with this fun craft made with a paper plate, hole punch, and string!

Markers (I used green, orange, red, yellow, and white)
1 heavy-duty paper plate
Hole punch
Scissors
54" of yarn
Tape
5–10 Paper Beads (see Paper Bead Necklace project in this chapter)
3–5 Feathers (see Feather Key Chain project in this chapter)
5–7 Colored Macaroni Noodles (optional) (see Macaroni Necklace project in this chapter)

1. Color the rim of your paper plate any way you would like. I used markers to make a random striped pattern of green, orange, red, yellow, and white.

2. Use the hole punch to punch holes every 1½" around the outside of the paper plate. Use the hole punch as a measuring tool to determine how far into the paper plate to punch a hole.

3. Use scissors to cut the center out of your paper plate, being careful to leave the rim intact. Use the natural line of the paper plate as a guide.

4. Thread a 24" piece of yarn up through the bottom of one of the holes that you punched in the plate, leaving about 2" of yarn hanging from the back of the plate. Secure the yarn with a piece of tape.

5. Use that yarn to create a spider web in the middle of the paper plate by threading the yarn randomly through the holes you punched in the plate. String Paper Beads onto the yarn as you weave your web. I used 6 Paper Beads for the center of the dream catcher.

6. To tie off the spider web, make sure the last string ends up in the hole next to the one that started the web. Remove the piece of tape, and tie the yarn together to hold the web in place. Be careful not to tie the yarn too tight, as doing so will warp your paper plate.

7. Now it is time to decorate your dream catcher. Cut an 8" piece of yarn and tie a Duct Tape Feather to the end. Then add a few pieces of Colored Macaroni Noodles and/or Paper Beads to the yarn. Make 3 strings and then tie the top of the yarn to 3 of the holes already in the bottom of the paper plate.

8. Loop a 6"-piece of yarn through the top two holes in the paper plate to make a simple hanger.

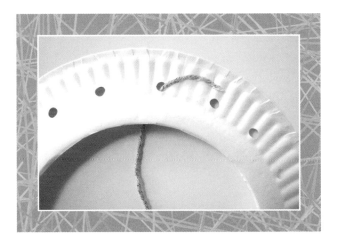

Fish

A single-hole punch proves to be one of my favorite crafting "machines" time and time again. I love that it's a two-for-one tool. With just one punch you get a perfectly round circle *and* a perfectly round punch in the paper. This hole-punch Fish is a fun art project because it utilizes what is typically the throwaway piece of the hole punch, the tiny round circle! This art work takes patience, but the kids will be very proud of their masterpieces when they see how all of the tiny holes come together to make a complete picture.

Pencil
1 notecard
Single-hole punch
4 sheets of colored paper (I used blue, orange, yellow, and white)

Egg carton
Glue
3—5 toothpicks
Black marker

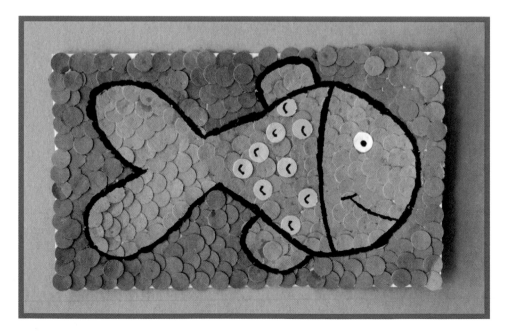

1. Draw a simple design onto a notecard with a pencil. I chose a fish, but any image will work!

2. Decide what color you want each part of your fish to be, then use the hole punch to punch holes in colored paper. For the fish, I punched out about 300 circles in my blue paper, 250 circles in my orange paper, 9 circles in my yellow paper, and 1 circle in my white paper. Sort the punched holes by color and divide them into an egg carton.

3. Cover a small area on the notecard in glue, and then use a toothpick to pick up a single punched-out hole and glue it to the notecard in the designated area. If you touch the toothpick to your tongue it will make picking up and placing the circles in their correct location so much easier!

4. Cover the entire notecard in punched-out holes to complete your image. Then with a black marker, outline the fish, give her a smile, and dot the white punched-out hole to give her a pupil and really make your fish come alive! Display your artwork with the Clothespin Art Displays from Chapter 2 to make your hole-punch art stand up anywhere!

KEEP IT CREATIVE!

This is a perfect project to do as a collaborative piece of art with multiple kids or even a classroom. Consider using a large piece of cardboard as the canvas, and let kids work together to complete one giant piece of art. It could even be done as an assembly line. Have a few kids punch specific colors of holes, one child spread glue, and a few kids actually do the dotting. It's all about team work!

Lacing Cards

Lacing cards are a great craft for older children to make for the younger kids. They are also a fun teaching tool for letters, shapes, and numbers, and help to refine young children's coordination skills. For older kids, lacing cards are a great way to introduce the basics of sewing!

Scissors
Cereal box
Pencil
Markers
Ruler
Hole punch
Tape
2 (24") pieces of yarn

1. Use scissors to cut a cereal box into 2 (4" × 6½") rectangles.

2. Decide what letters, shapes, or pictures you want to use to decorate your cards. I choose a "J" and "D" because those are my initials.

3. With a pencil, draw your letters on the front of the rectangles. Then use a marker to make the line thick and bold.

4. Use a ruler and a pencil to mark where you want to punch your holes. I punched the holes 1" apart in the middle of the bold letters I drew.

5. Use the hole punch to punch out the holes! You might have to fold your rectangle to maneuver your hole punch into the middle of the card.

6. Use a marker to decorate the front side of the lacing cards with stars or other shapes and patterns.

7. Use a small piece of tape to cover the ends of the yarn and start stringing!

Lion Mask

Lions and tigers and bears, oh my! Kids will love that this Lion Mask has a touch-and-feel mane and, after the craft is made, the kids can create a short skit that involves the other masks in the book. I can see the plot unfolding already: Super Maxwell (wearing the duct tape Superhero Mask from earlier in this chapter) and Leo in the Lion Mask save Pete in the Panda Mask (Chapter 2) from the giant with his scary Monster Feet (Chapter 4)!

Paintbrush
1 paper plate
Paint (I used orange)
Hole punch
Ruler
Yarn (I used orange and light yellow)
Scissors
Colored paper (I used yellow and orange)
Glue
Black marker
Packing tape
Paint stir stick

1. Use a paintbrush to paint the front side of the paper plate orange. Let the paper plate dry according to package instructions.

2. Once the plate is dry, use your hole punch to punch holes every inch or so around the perimeter of the plate.

3. Use a ruler to measure and cut 1 (9½") piece of yarn per hole that was punched. It's best if all of the yarn is the same length. I alternated between 2 different colors of yarn.

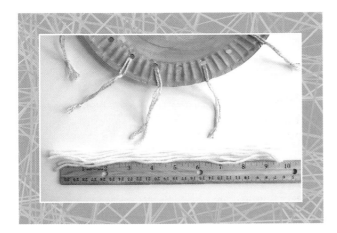

4. Tie each piece of yarn into a loop, and hook it through the holes in the paper plate. (Actually, you can tie the yarn any way you'd like. I'm just telling you how I did it!)

5. Cut a 6" round circle out of yellow paper, and glue it to the center of your paper plate.

6. Cut 2 triangles to use as ears and 6 long, skinny rectangles to use as whiskers out of your orange paper.

7. Use a black marker to draw on a face, then glue the ears and whiskers into place.

8. Use clear packing tape to attach the paint stir stick to the mask, and enjoy!

Tie-Dye Shoelaces

Tie-Dye Shoelaces make any pair of shoes instantly more fun! Any age kid (and even some adults) will love turning their plain white shoelaces into a groovy masterpiece. Best of all, you can make this craft with a few simple things you likely have in your home right now, including Sharpie markers, rubbing alcohol, and cotton swabs. Oh, and of course a pair of white shoelaces!

White shoelaces
1 brown paper bag
Sharpie markers (I used blue, pink, orange, and yellow)
1 cotton swab
Rubbing alcohol

1. Lay the white shoelaces on a brown paper bag. Doodle lines and dots onto both shoelaces with Sharpie markers. Cover 90–100 percent of the shoelaces with color.

2. Dip a cotton swab into the rubbing alcohol and drip onto the covered shoelaces until each shoelace has been completely covered in rubbing alcohol. I like to do the shoelaces in about 4" sections.

3. Let the shoelaces dry overnight, and then re-lace into your sneakers for a funky new look!

Faux Stained Glass

Stained glass is a beautiful art form that many kids probably don't see on a daily basis. Kids will love inventing their very own stained glass designs with yarn and coloring them in with permanent markers! When they're done, these are fun to hang in a child's dollhouse, display on the fridge, or even display using the Clothespin Art Display from Chapter 2.

Cereal box
Scissors
Pencil
2 (20") pieces of yarn per 2 Faux Stained Glass windows
Glue
Tin foil
Permanent markers (I used blue, red, green, and black)

1. Disassemble your cereal box by gently ripping the seams on the side and bottom of the box with your finger.

2. Cut one side of the cereal box off with your scissors so that you have a large square. My squares are 5" × 5" squares.

3. Use a pencil to draw a simple design onto the blank side of the cereal box. Cut pieces of yarn to cover your simple design.

4. Cover the design in glue and adhere the yarn to the cardboard.

5. Let it dry completely, and then cover the cardboard with tin foil, making sure the yarn can be easily seen. Use your fingers to press the tin foil around the yarn so that you can see the yarn bump. If the tin foil rips, just cover it with another layer of foil.

6. Color the inside of the yarn shapes with permanent markers. Then color the raised parts of the tin foil with a black permanent marker.

Awesome Facts

Stained glass windows are beautiful and date back to the ancient times of the Egyptians and Romans. These Faux Stained Glass windows are a great way to introduce kids to this beautiful art form.

Macaroni Necklace

This project is a modern version of a classic kid craft, the noodle necklace! This version is just as easy to make, but with the addition of permanent markers and a unique stringing method, this necklace is a real show-stopper. Little entrepreneurs will be selling Macaroni Necklaces to the entire neighborhood in no time!

Colored Macaroni Noodles
Permanent marker (I used red)
Penne pasta

Macaroni Necklace
Scissors
24" piece of string

1. **For Colored Macaroni Noodles:** Use a permanent marker to color your penne pasta noodles. I used 6 noodles per necklace.

KEEP IT CREATIVE!

I chose to make a monotone Macaroni Necklace, but consider using a different color for each noodle, or even draw designs, doodles, and words on your noodles. The possibilities are endless. Also, I used 6 noodles, but this necklace can be made with as many noodles as you would like!

2. **For Macaroni Necklace:** String on 1 penne pasta noodle just a few inches onto the string.

3. Grab the other end of your string and pull that string through the opposite end of the noodle.

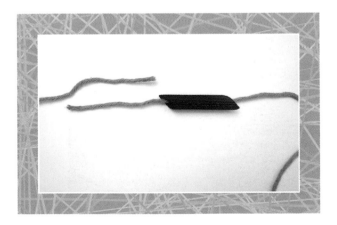

4. String 4 more noodles onto the string using this method.

5. Add a sixth noodle to one side of the string and then loop the same side of the string through the noodle.

6. Tie the strings together in a simple knot after ensuring that the necklace can fit over your head.

Sun Catchers

Give a plastic milk jug new life as a Sun Catcher with this fun kid craft! Kids will enjoy making the craft and then seeing their handiwork glow in the window. High five to sunshine and recycling!

Scissors
1 (1-gallon) plastic milk jug
Permanent markers (I used orange, blue, yellow, and black)
3–5" round stencil (from either a glass or candle)

1. Use scissors to cut the top narrow portion of the plastic milk jug off so that you are left with 4 flat sides and a bottom.

2. Cut the remaining milk jug into 4 plastic sheets. You will not use the bottom part of the milk jug.

3. Use a black permanent marker and your stencil of choice to trace as many round circles onto the plastic sheets as you can. Typically, you can get 4-5 (3") circles from the plastic milk jug. Once your circles are cut, use permanent markers to make suns on your sun catcher. Add black permanent marker outlines to a few of your suns to really make them stand out!

Festive Garland

Whether your child has a blank bedroom wall or a classroom party to decorate for, this project is a fun and easy way to spiff up any space. Kids will love helping you prepare for a party by creating these fun, festive garlands full of pattern and color. This is another craft that is fun for multiple kids to work on together. Each child can complete 1 notecard, and then you can string them together to make an extra-long Festive Garland!

Markers (I used green, orange, red, and yellow)
At least 5 notecards

Hole punch
36" of yarn or string

1. Use colored markers to cover the front side of at least 5 notecards. Try different patterns, doodles, and designs. Each notecard can be totally different!

2. Punch 2 holes in the top of each notecard, and use a piece of yarn to string all of the notecards together.

Postcard

Snail mail gives kids a chance to practice their handwriting and grammar skills, but they won't even notice you're giving them a lesson because these are so fun to craft! Have your kids send these fun Postcards to long-distance relatives and friends to stay in touch.

2 notecards per Postcard
Markers
Ruler
Glue

1. Cover the blank side of one notecard with marker. I wrote a simple message with a black marker, and then did a zigzag design around each letter. I continued this pattern until the entire notecard was filled with color.

2. On the blank side of the other notecard, use a ruler to measure 4" from the left-hand side of the card. Draw a line at that 4" mark to divide the notecard into 2 sections.

3. On the right side of the notecard with the line write the recipient's full address.

4. To actually send the Postcard, you will need to use a certified postcard stamp from the post office, but for fun you can doodle a stamp in the upper right hand corner of the postcard with a black pen like I did!

5. On the left hand side of the notecard write a little note to your loved one.

6. Glue the blank sides of the notecards together and get it ready to mail!

Awesome Fact

The first postcard was sent in 1840 to a writer named Theodore Hook from London, England. Some people think that he actually sent the postcard to himself!

Altered Scrapbook

Scrapbooks are a great way to preserve memories, but traditional scrapbooking is time-consuming, expensive, and tough for little kids to do. Here's a super-easy alternative that the kids can make and you can all enjoy looking at for years to come. It's also a great way to remember a specific event, such as a birthday party, vacation, or school year!

50+ page hardcover book
Glue
Water
Sponge brush
Wax paper

Pictures and memorabilia
Scissors
Magazines
A variety of colored paper

1. First, determine how many pages you want in your altered scrapbook. I recommend about 1 scrapbook page per 20 numbered book pages (you will be gluing groups of 10 pages together for sturdiness). So if the book you are using has 60 physical pages/120 numbered pages, you will end up with a 6-page scrapbook.

2. Make your glue mixture: Add 1 part glue to 1 part water and stir together. It's easiest to empty 1 bottle of white school glue into a bowl and fill the empty bottle with water. Stir the mixture together. This will make the pages smooth and not wrinkle as much.

3. Dip a sponge brush into the glue mixture to glue 10 physical book pages together. This will form thick, sturdy pages for your altered scrapbook. Place a sheet of wax paper in between the newly created altered book pages so that they do not stick together from excess glue.

4. Let your altered book pages dry overnight.

5. Now it's time for the fun part: decorating your scrapbook pages with memorabilia! You can use ticket stubs from movies, amusement parks, shows, concerts, or airlines. Or cut out sayings or pictures you like from greeting cards, calendars, or magazines. Printed photographs are also a great addition to altered books. Some other fun ideas include polka dots made with a hole punch, newspaper clippings, stickers, quotes, or any traditional scrapbook materials you might already have on hand.

6. Consider giving each altered book a theme. Maybe it's your son's eighth birthday party or a family vacation at the beach or even just second grade! Whatever you choose, you can use that for ideas about how to decorate your pages. For a summer theme, for example, you could make suns out of construction paper and place a photo in the center of each.

Trees

Typically books are made out of trees, but this creative craft switches things up! My amazing mom, Terri Smith, is the creative genius behind this fun craft. When I was growing up, my mom and I made these Trees at Christmas time to use as centerpieces for the dining room table. I think they would also be a great addition to the masking tape Race Track earlier in this chapter!

Scissors
150 page+ paperback book per tree
4–5 paper clips per tree
24" of string per tree
Colored Macaroni Noodles (see Macaroni Necklace project in this chapter) (optional)
Single-hole punch (optional)
Colored paper (optional)
1 pipe cleaner per tree

1. Tear or use scissors to cut the front and back covers off of the book.

2. Next, fold each page in the book: Start with the first page and fold the top right corner to the center of the binding. Then fold the bottom right corner up ½".

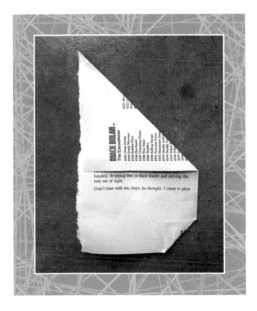

3. Then with the same page, fold the entire page diagonally in toward the binding. Continue folding every single page in the book this way.

4. Once all of your pages are folded, fold your book into a cone shape, and use 4–5 paper clips to secure the front and back pages in the book to each other so that the book holds its cone shape.

5. Decorate your trees with string and Colored Macaroni Noodles, or construction paper and a hole punch, or anything else that you can think up. You can secure the macaroni noodle garland to your paper tree with paper clips or tape. Punched-out holes can be glued to the tree.

6. Finally, shape a single pipe cleaner into a star shape and stick the end inside of the top of the tree!

Envelope

This craft wins the prize for most useful and easiest craft in the entire book! I love sending snail mail cards, and I certainly want to instill the love of handwritten notes in my own kids. A magazine page envelope is a simple way to make a handwritten note that much more special and personalized. Part of the fun of this craft involves flipping through magazines to find the perfect magazine page for the snail mail recipient! This is a craft you and the kids will make again and again.

Scissors
1 magazine page
Clear tape
Masking tape or a notecard or mailing labels

1. Cut your magazine page into a square using scissors. Typically you can get at least an 8" × 8" square out of the magazine page.

2. Lay the square in front of you like a diamond, with a point facing you. Fold the bottom point up. Then fold the points on the left and right to the center and secure them with tape.

3. Fill the envelope with a handmade card, cereal box puzzle, or letter and seal with a piece of tape!

4. If you have adhesive mailing labels on hand, awesome! Stick 2 labels on the front of the envelope to use as a mailing label and a return address.

KEEP IT CREATIVE!

Don't have mailing labels on hand? No worries. I like to use washi tape or masking tape as the address and return address labels.

Paper Bead Necklace

Kids will love that they can turn a simple stack of magazines into beads! And once the paper beads are made, you can use them to make a variety of necklaces, bracelets, and key chains galore. I also used them to decorate the Dream Catcher earlier in this chapter. Let the paper beading begin!

Paper Beads
Scissors
Magazine
Pencil or chopstick; anything with
  a tapered end will work
Glue

Paper Bead Necklace
50" of string

1. For Paper Beads: Cut strips of 1 magazine page into long triangular-shaped pieces that are 8" long.

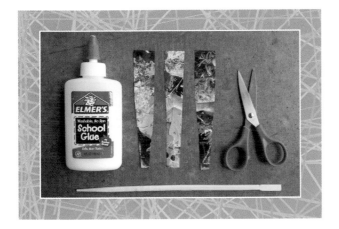

2. Place the wide end of the triangular piece of magazine around the tapered end of your chopstick. Begin to roll the triangular piece of magazine page around the tapered end of the chopstick, squirting small amounts of glue as you roll. Use as little glue as possible; you do not want the magazine page to stick to the chopstick.

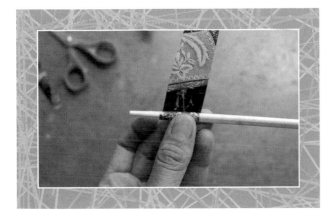

3. Roll all 8" of the magazine page around itself, using as little glue as possible. Gently slide the bead off of the chopstick and allow the bead at least an hour to dry.

4. Once the bead is completely dry, use scissors to cut the cylinder-shaped bead into smaller pieces to make multiple beads. You can make your beads as long or short as you would like. For my necklace, I cut each cylinder into 3 equal parts.

5. For Paper Bead Necklace: Find the center of your string and tie a knot about 6" to the right of the center of the string. Tie 4–5 knots in one place. The goal of this large knot is to keep your paper beads from going past the knot.

6. String 1 bead and tie 4–5 more knots in the string to keep the bead in one spot. Then string another bead, and do the same process of stringing and knotting for the remaining 4 paper beads.

KEEP IT CREATIVE!

You can create paper beads with almost any kind of paper including construction paper, white printer paper colored with markers, newspaper, and book pages. Experiment and get creative! Consider making a few necklaces like this and layering them around your neck for a fun new look.

Ziptop Bag Sheep

Bah, bah, black sheep, have you any wool? Yes sir, yes sir, 3 ziptop bags full! And while you don't exactly have wool in your Ziptop Bag Sheep, this craft encourages kids to think outside the box. Ask your kids what materials they think would make a good wool alternative to put in the bag. Anything white in appearance, such as cotton balls, toilet paper, or rice, is a great suggestion!

1 ziptop bag
Shredded mostly white paper
Scissors
2 sheets of paper (I used black and white)
Glue
Black marker
Stapler

1. Fill the ziptop bag with shredded paper. When the bag is full, zip up the bag!

2. The sheep's face is made out of 5 ovals. Cut 1 large 4"-long black oval for the face and 2 smaller 3"-long black ovals for ears. Then, cut 2 even smaller 1"-long white ovals to be used as eyes for the sheep.

3. Cut out 4 long, skinny rectangles out of black construction paper; these will be the sheep's legs. My rectangles are about 2½" × ½".

4. Glue the 2 small black ovals to the back of the large black oval. These will be the sheep's ears. Glue them on the top about 1" apart so that the majority of the ears stick out to the side of the oval, facing downward.

5. Glue the small white ovals to the front of the sheep's face, about 1" from the top of the head, to create the sheep's eyes. Use a black marker to draw in pupils.

6. Turn your ziptop bag so that the zip is on the bottom, and insert the 4 legs into the opening. Seal the bag.

7. Staple the sheep's head to the top right of the ziptop bag, and "ewe" have got yourself an adorable little sheep!

KEEP IT CREATIVE!

If you have a paper shredder in your home, perfect! You will just use the shredded paper from the bin as needed. If you don't have a paper shredder, you can shred paper with your hands or cut into strips with scissors! Try to use junk mail or paper that would typically be thrown away to avoid making excess trash.

Thumbtack Ghost Pumpkins

This is an awesome, mess-free, and inexpensive way to decorate pumpkins with a large group of kids, who will love that they can "carve" a pumpkin all by themselves. And you will love that the messy guts of the pumpkins and danger of using knives are not issues. Explain to the kids that they can gently push thumbtacks into the pumpkin to make ghosts or faces, patterns, letters, or pictures. The pumpkins are sure to turn out *gourd*-geous no matter what!

Permanent marker
1 carving pumpkin (you can use any pumpkin except those really tiny ones)
Thumbtacks (I used white)

1. Use the marker to outline a simple ghost shape on your pumpkin, then place the white thumbtacks on the marker outline.

2. Use the white thumbtacks to fill in the outline. It's okay if the tacks overlap each other.

3. When your ghost is all filled in, use the marker to color 3 of the tacks black and stick them into the pumpkin to use as the ghost's eyes.

KEEP IT CREATIVE!

Want to keep your thumbtack ghost pumpkin for next year? Use a foam pumpkin from the craft store to ensure that your pumpkin doesn't rot!

Matching Game

As a 4-year-old child I could beat my dad at the game of Memory! I still love this game, and know that your kids will enjoy making their very own personalized memory cards with pictures that they created themselves. The only rule to this craft is that there needs to be matching pairs, so the child must draw 2 similar pictures on 2 separate cards. Of course, after the game is made, be prepared to play 1,000 rounds of this Matching Game!

1 colored pocket folder (or notebook cover)
Scissors
Ruler
Pencil
Colored markers

1. Use your fingers to rip open the seams of the interior pockets of your folder, then cut the pockets off completely.

2. Open the folder and lay it flat so that it is face up. Then mark 2" intervals lengthwise. Use a pencil and ruler to draw a straight line at each interval, and use scissors to cut your folder into 2"-wide strips.

3. Mark 2" intervals on each strip and use scissors to cut each strip into 2" × 2" squares. One folder will make about 40 squares.

4. Decorate each square with colored markers. Remember it's a matching game, so it's important to have 2 of the same square. Your memory game can be themed or be a collection of fun doodles and pictures that your kids enjoy drawing. Animals, transportation, nature, and shapes are a few fun themes to get you started!

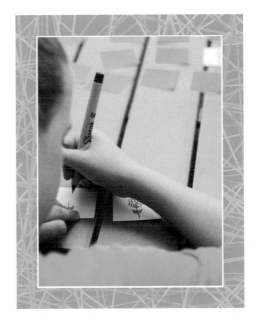

Rubber Band Desk Organizer

Vanessa Brady at *www.triedandtrueblog.com* created this craft with the help of her 2 sons. They needed more storage for their art supplies, and Vanessa wanted the boys to help solve the problem. Rubber bands proved to be a very easy material for little hands to maneuver, and together they created this one-of-a-kind, modern desk organizer that your kids will love as much as hers do!

> **Tin can with label removed (since the entire tin can is going to be covered in rubber bands, it is okay if a little of the label is left)**
> **25—30 rubber bands of varying colors**

1. Clean out a tin can and let it dry completely.

2. Position rubber bands around the tin can in a pattern. I chose to do a simple pattern with the rubber bands: pink, purple, green, blue. Pink, purple, green, blue.

KEEP IT CREATIVE!

While the instructions and photos for this project show the rubber bands placed on the can in a pattern, feel free to let your kids get creative. They can place the rubber bands on the can at random or use a pattern. Have them use whatever color rubber bands they want or let them create a monotone can if that's what they choose!

3. Place on your desk and use as a catch-all for pens and other art supplies!

Chapter 4

BATHROOM

Hair ties, cotton swabs, tissue boxes, and toilet paper tubes may not appear to be very crafty—until you add paint, scissors, and permanent markers to the mix! Empty toilet paper tubes are so fun because they allow kids to wear and interact with their creations, since the cardboard tubes can stand up on their own (as with the Toilet Paper Roll animals) or be worn around a wrist (as with the Watch and Bracelet projects). You'll also use hair ties to create Sponge Balls and a Ribbon Wand, and cotton swabs—well, those little guys are absolutely amazing "free" paintbrushes! So go raid your bathroom for craft supplies and start creating some really awesome bathroom crafts!

Watch

Tick tock, tick tock goes the crafting clock! Hurry—you might run out of time to make this craft! Kids will love that they get to craft and wear a "real" watch just like Mom and Dad. It's also a great conversation starter about time and how a clock face works.

Scissors
1 empty toilet paper roll
1 notecard

Pencil
Black permanent marker
1 brad

1. Use your scissors to cut a 1½"-wide (or however wide you want your watchband) piece off of an empty toilet paper roll.

2. Make a single cut in the toilet paper roll tube so that the watch will slip on over any size wrist.

3. From the leftover toilet paper roll tube, cut 2 small triangles, to be used as hands. One triangle should be a little bit smaller than the other. The hands should be approximately ½" and ¼" long.

4. Use the remainder of the empty toilet paper roll to trace a round circle onto a notecard with a pencil. Cut out the circle. This will be the face of your watch.

5. Use a black marker to draw numbers on the watch face and decorate your watchband. Also use it to outline the circle of the watch face, and add black marker to the tips of the watch hands.

6. Use the pointy end of the scissors to poke a hole in each of your watch pieces: the 2 hands, the watch face, and the band. The holes should be in the center of each of the pieces.

7. Sandwich all 4 items together and connect them with a brad. Put the watch on your wrist and set the time!

Awesome Fact

Did you know that pocket watches were way more popular than wrist watches until the 1920s? And that before then, men almost exclusively used pocket watches while women wore wristwatches?

Bracelet

Toilet paper roll bracelets are a great addition to the watch. They add a pop of color, and complete the party on your wrist! You can make these bracelets any width, and liven them up by using different colors of yarn.

Scissors
1 empty toilet paper roll
60" of yarn

1. Cut a 2"-wide piece off of an empty toilet paper roll. (You can make the bracelet any width you want by cutting the toilet paper roll to size as needed.)

2. Make a single cut in the toilet paper roll tube so that the bracelet will slip over any size wrist.

3. Cut ¼" slits in the top and bottom of the toilet paper roll right next to the opening for your wrist. This is where you will start the yarn to wrap around the bracelet. Make the same cuts on the other side of the opening.

4. Insert the yarn into the slit and tie a knot on the inside of the bracelet. Place the tail of the yarn on the inside of the band and being wrapping the yarn around the toilet paper roll, being sure to cover the tail as you continue to wrap.

5. Once the yarn has been wrapped around the entire bracelet, insert the yarn into the slits like you did in the beginning, and tie a knot. Tie the knot on the inside of the bracelet and cut off the tail.

Toilet Paper Roll Owl

Turn a spent toilet paper tube into an adorable owl! The kids will love the creative process of using what they know as trash to craft a feathered friend. Once the owl (and the other 4 toilet paper roll friends in this chapter) are made, your kids can enjoy playing pretend with all of their new critters.

1 toilet paper roll
Cereal box
Black marker
Lid from 1 plastic milk jug
Scissors
Glue

1. Use your finger to press down the top of one side of the empty toilet paper roll. Then press down the other side to make 2 points. These will be the owl's ears.

2. Disassemble your cereal box by gently ripping the seams on the side and bottom of the box with your finger.

3. On the back side of the cereal box, use a black marker to trace a circle around your milk jug lid. Add 2 triangles at the top of the circle for the owl's ears. Use your scissors to cut out the circle and the ears as one piece.

4. Use the black marker to draw 2 large round eyes and a triangle for a beak onto the circle.

5. With the black marker, draw 2 wing shapes on the toilet paper tube. This is as simple as drawing 2 lines to form a 45° angle on either side of the tube, about 1" from the bottom.

6. Use a pair of scissors to cut into the toilet paper tube and cut along the lines you drew to form the wings so that the wings stay attached, but pop out.

7. Draw some simple dots and lines on the owl's belly and add 2 feet at the bottom.

8. Glue the Owl's head onto the top of the toilet paper roll, and allow the glue to dry according to the package instructions.

Toilet Paper Roll Deer

Oh deer, this is an adorable craft made out of an empty toilet paper roll. Living in Texas, we have deer spottings frequently, and even my 1-year-old son gets really excited! I know your animal-loving kiddos will love making this deer craft just as much as mine do.

1 toilet paper roll
Cereal box
Black marker
Scissors
Glue
White piece of paper

1. Use your finger to press down the top of one side of the empty toilet paper roll. Then press down the other side to make 2 points.

2. Disassemble your cereal box by gently ripping the seams on the side and bottom of the box with your finger.

3. On the back side of the cereal box, use a black marker to draw a 1½"-long triangle. Then round the triangle's corners to form the shape of the deer's head. Make 2 ears, 1 on the end of each of the rounded triangle corners. Then draw 2 antlers that come out from the ears. The antlers can be as big as you would like. I made mine about 1"-long each.

4. Cut out the deer's head with scissors and glue the head to the top of the toilet paper roll.

5. Cut a small oval out of the white piece of paper and glue it just under the deer's head to create the deer's belly.

Toilet Paper Roll Lion

This super-simple toilet paper roll lion is easy and perfect for making after you watch *The Lion King* or read *The Happy Lion* by Louise Fatio. If your kid-do is really into lions, don't forget about the lion mask in Chapter 3!

Cereal box
Black marker
Scissors
Glue
Clothespin clamp (optional)
1 toilet paper roll

1. Disassemble your cereal box by gently ripping the seams on the side and bottom of the box with your finger.

2. On the back side of the cereal box, use a black marker to draw a 2" oval. Then draw a 2½" oval around your first oval. At the top of the inside oval draw 2 rounded ears. The ears should be drawn in the area between the 2 ovals. Then, in the center of the inside oval, draw on 2 eyes, a nose, a mouth, and whiskers.

3. Cut out the lion's head and glue it to the top half of the toilet paper roll. This is where a clothespin clamp might come in handy to secure the head to the toilet paper roll without having to hold it with your hands.

4. Draw 2 front legs onto the front of the toilet paper roll with a black marker. Start about 1" under the lion's head and draw 2 sets of parallel lines that reach the bottom of the cardboard tube. Then add 3 tiny black lines to each paw to represent toes.

5. To make the lion's tail, use the black marker to draw 2 parallel, squiggly lines. Then cut along the lines. Be careful not to cut the tail completely off of the tube when you reach the top. Next, fold the tail up so it shows from the front of the lion, then color in the tip of the tail with the black marker.

Awesome Fact

The roar of a lion can be heard from 5 miles away! Wow!

Toilet Paper Roll Bear

Your kids are guaranteed to growl with delight at this Toilet Paper Roll Bear. The bear's head is just a round circle, the arm cutouts are small and simple, and the bear's face is made up of only 3 black dots. How easy is that? The kids are going to love playing pretend with their new friend!

Cereal box
Black marker
Lid from 1 plastic milk jug
Scissors
Glue
Toilet paper roll
1 piece of white paper

1. Disassemble your cereal box by gently ripping the seams on the side and bottom of the box with your finger.

2. On the back side of the cereal box, use a black marker to trace a circle around a milk jug lid. Add 2 oval ears at the top of the circle for the bear's ears. Cut out the bear's face as one piece.

3. Use a black marker to draw 2 black dots for eyes and an oval for a nose. Color the inside of the bear's ears black. Then glue the bear's face to the top of the toilet paper roll.

4. Once the face is glued on, use a black marker to draw 2 small, ½" ovals for arms. Cut out the arm holes using scissors, leaving a small portion at the top of the arm attached to the toilet paper roll.

5. Cut an oval out of a white piece of paper and glue it to the front center of the toilet paper roll to represent the bear's belly.

Toilet Paper Roll Monkey

All kids love banana-eating, tree-swinging, fun-loving monkeys! It would be fun to watch or read about Curious George before you make this craft, but either way I am positive that your kids will go bananas for this Toilet Paper Roll Monkey craft!

Cereal box
Black marker
Scissors
Glue
Toilet paper roll
Colored paper (I used yellow)

1. Disassemble your cereal box by gently ripping the seams on the side and bottom of the box with your finger.

2. On the back side of the cereal box, use a black marker to draw a 1½" horizontal oval. Add 2 half circles to either side of the oval for the monkey's ears. Use your scissors to cut out the monkey's face as one piece.

3. Use a black marker to draw a monkey face onto the oval you cut out in the previous step. First you need to draw a semicircle on the bottom of the monkey's face. The semicircle should start where the black outline meets the bottom of the ear and curve upward to meet the bottom of the other ear. Two simple black dots work perfectly for the eyes; draw a curved line to outline the eyes.

4. Glue the face onto the top of the toilet paper roll, then allow to dry according to package instructions. Once the monkey's face is dry, use a black marker to draw 2 (1½"-long) skinny monkey arms on the toilet paper roll tube. The arms should start right underneath the monkey's head and curve outward until about 1" from the bottom of the toilet paper tube. Using scissors, cut out the arms, leaving a small portion of the arm attached at the top of the toilet paper tube.

5. Cut a banana shape out of the yellow paper and glue the banana to the monkey's hand. Then use a black marker to draw a 1½" oval onto the monkey's belly and enjoy your newest menagerie member!

KEEP IT CREATIVE!

To make these toilet paper roll creatures into puppets, just glue or tape a Popsicle stick to the inside of the toilet paper roll and let the puppet show games begin!

Lighted Garland

Jennifer Perkins at *http://jenniferperkins.com* created this one-of-a-kind lighted garland with the help of her daughter. They used toilet paper roll tubes as mini lantern covers and decorated them with tissue paper to give her daughter a functionally beautiful reading light in her bedroom. Kids will love that they can use their very own lighted garland in forts or above their bed for nighttime reading.

Scissors
10–15 toilet paper rolls
Hole punch
Small bowl or drinking glass
White globe string lights with 15 light bulbs
Nonflammable glue or decoupage medium such as Mod Podge
Tissue paper (You can use any color or pattern—Jennifer found a really fun flower-patterned tissue paper for this craft!)
Paintbrush
Washi tape (optional)
Paint (Jennifer used blue) (optional)

1. Cut each toilet paper tube into 3 equal sections. You will need a section for each bulb on your string lights.

2. Use your hole punch to punch a hole in the center of each tube section. This is where you will insert the top portion of the globe lights.

3. Use a template (small bowl or drinking glass) that is slightly larger than the end of your tube section and trace circles onto your tissue paper. You will need 2 circles for each tube.

4. Insert the bulbs from the string lights into the tubes. You will need to unscrew each light bulb to fit the top portion of the light bulb through the hole and then screw the light bulb back into the socket inside of the new shade.

5. Using glue or decoupage medium, apply a thin layer to the top of the toilet paper tube piece. Then lay your circular pieces of tissue paper over the end of the cardboard tube and use a paint-brush (or your finger) to press the tissue paper overlap over the end of the toilet paper roll and ensure that it sticks.

6. After your glue dries, decorate the rest of the toilet paper tubes. Washi tape and paint are great options.

7. Help your kiddo string up the lights and enjoy a bedtime story by your handmade lanterns!

KEEP IT CREATIVE!

It's best to buy LED strand lights that are not a fire hazard. Some globe string lights (especially bargain-store brands) can be dangerous, so make sure yours are safe before using in this craft. If you're unsure about the safety of your materials, consider using safer, brand-name LED lights instead.

Ribbon Wand

Dance parties are a big hit in our house! Add a Ribbon Wand and you'll have a choreographed dance performance happening in no time. You'll need at least 1 Ribbon Wand per family member. I also suggest adding the Turtle Shaker and the Drum from Chapter 2 for a little variety on family music night!

Permanent markers (I used a variety of bright colored ones)
3—5 (18") pieces of smooth white ribbon
Brown paper bag
2—5 cotton swabs
Rubbing alcohol
1 hair tie
10—15 (18") pieces of solid-colored ribbon

1. Use different colored permanent markers to doodle all over the white ribbons. Try different techniques and include stripes, zigzags, lines, polka dots, words, shapes—anything goes! The only rule is to cover the white ribbon in colorful markers.

2. Place the ribbons on a brown paper bag for the next, messy stage. Dip a cotton swab into the alcohol container and drip onto the white ribbon. Repeat until all 5 ribbons are completed. Watch the colors instantly swirl together.

3. Give the ribbons about 1 hour to dry completely. Then tie each ribbon onto the hair tie with a simple knot.

4. Finally, tie the solid-colored ribbons in between the tie-dyed ribbons, and get the party started!

Sponge Balls

These are fun to make and even more fun to play with outside on a hot summer day. The kids will love that sponge balls are made to get wet! Use them to toss to each other, to learn to juggle, or to toss into buckets filled with water.

Scissors
4 colorful 4–5"-long sponges (this will make 5 balls)
5 hair ties

1. Cut each sponge into 5 equal pieces. Each piece should be about ¾" wide.

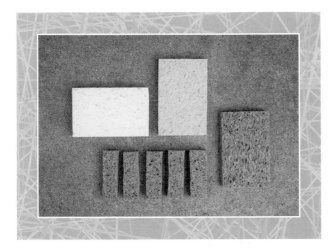

2. If using different colored sponges, take 1 piece of each color and stack them on top of each other. Fan them out so that you can see every piece.

3. Put the stack of sponges through the hair tie, and wrap the hair tie 3 times around the middle of the sponge stack.

4. Once the hair tie is secured, manipulate your sponge balls so they have a nice round form. Beware: Sponges can tear, so do not yank on an individual piece of sponge too hard.

Sushi

Sushi is a Japanese dish that typically consists of cooked rice, seafood, and vegetables. If your kids enjoy cooking in the kitchen, this craft is a fun way to introduce them to new foods. They will love crafting up their sushi pieces and learning how to use chopsticks!

Scissors
A few 1" scraps of fabric or ribbon
Scraps of colored paper (I used orange)
2 cotton balls per piece of sushi
Black tape (washi or electrical)

1. Gather your materials together and cut up your fabric, ribbon, and colored paper scraps into 1"-long strips.

2. To make a piece of sushi, take 5 pieces of 1" strips of ribbon, colored paper, and/or fabric and sandwich them between 2 cotton balls. Let about ¼" of the colorful "filling" poke out between the side-by-side cotton balls.

3. Wrap the black tape around the cotton balls multiple times to hold everything together. Wrap the tape just tightly enough to hold everything together; you want the sushi pieces to be nice and cylinder in shape.

Water Bottle Polar Bear

There are lots of fun polar bear books to go along with this craft, including *On the Night You Were Born* and *Polar Bear, Polar Bear, What Do You Hear?* Kids will love crafting up this adorable Water Bottle Polar Bear while wearing the Panda Mask project found in Chapter 2!

Empty (12-ounce) plastic water
  bottle, dry, with label removed
Cotton balls
Pencil
1 notecard
Scissors
Black marker
Glue or tape

1. Fill the clean, dry water bottle with cotton balls.

2. Use a pencil to draw 1 (5") large circle for the polar bear's face onto the notecard. Add 2 (1"-wide) half circles to the top portion of the large circle to act as the polar bear's ears. Cut out the face and ears using scissors.

3. Next, draw the eyes, mouth, and nose with a black marker. Glue or tape the head to the very top of the plastic bottle.

Awesome Fact

Polar Bear paws can measure up to 1 foot in diameter! Their paws are so big to help distribute the weight on thin ice.

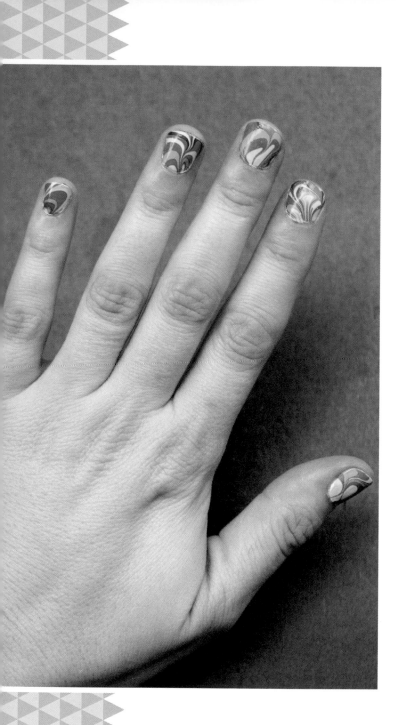

Tie-Dye Manicure

Yes, with this project, you can craft a tie-dye manicure onto your nails, and it is really not that hard! This craft project is brought to you by my friend Annie McBroom. She has been tie-dying nails of all of our friends and friends' kids for many moons. This is a project that will absolutely need some adult assistance, but I have a feeling you too will end up with psychedelic nails (and love it).

Tape
White nail polish
A wide-mouth cup filled with room
   temperature water
5 colors of nail polish (Annie used yellow,
   orange, pink, purple, and blue)
Toothpicks
Paper towels
Nail polish remover
5—10 cotton swabs

1. Place tape around the edges of each fingernail. This makes for easier cleanup later.

2. Paint all of your nails with white nail polish. Having a white base makes the tie-dye pattern and colors really pop.

3. Take your cup of room temperature water and add 1 drop of nail polish at a time to the water. You want to create a bull's-eye effect on the surface of the water. If the nail polish drop falls to the bottom of the cup, dump your water out and start again, but without the polish that sunk. This just means that that particular color and brand of nail polish will not work for the Tie-Dye Manicure.

4. Gently drag and swirl a toothpick through the bull's-eye of nail polish to create designs.

5. Find a section of design you want on your nail and dunk your nail into the water, making sure that your fingernail is facing down and is parallel to the water's surface so that the design will stick to your nail.

6. Once your nail is in the water, straighten your finger and lift it straight out of the water. Take a toothpick and swirl in the water to remove all of the leftover polish. Polish will form a ball on the end of your toothpick; just wipe it off on a paper towel. Note: You'll need to remove the nail polish from the water after you tie-dye each nail, but the polish will form a ball and come out of the water easily.

7. Repeat steps 3 through 6 for each of your 10 nails.

8. When your nails are complete and dry, remove the clear tape and use nail polish remover and cotton swabs to clean up around each of your nails.

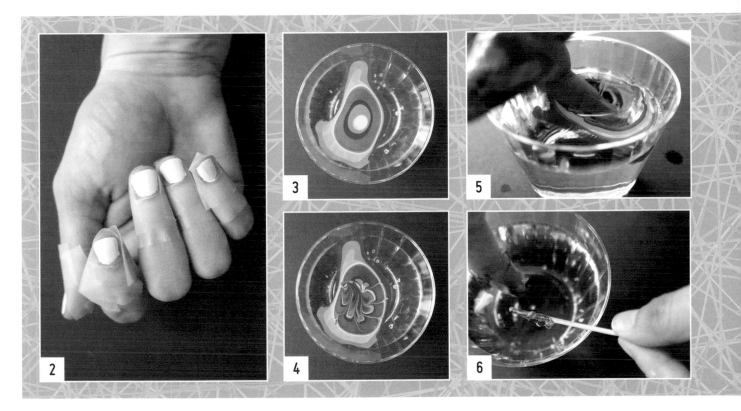

Cactus Dot Painting

Pointillism is a painting technique that uses small dots of colors in precise patterns to form a picture. That's exactly what your kids are going to do with a cotton swab, paint, and a notecard. Oh, and this is a great craft to utilize the Clothespin Art Display project from Chapter 2 so that their artwork can be proudly displayed anywhere in the house!

Pencil
1 notecard
1 cotton swab per color
   (I used 4)
Paint (I used light blue,
   dark blue, green, and
   brown)
Black marker

1. First, use a pencil to draw a simple picture of a cactus onto the blank side of a notecard.

KEEP IT CREATIVE!

This technique works best if you create 1 large picture like a single cactus (as seen here). Some other fun ideas include a tree, flower, sun, car, airplane, ladybug, or fish!

2. Dip a cotton swab into the desired color of paint and dot it onto your picture.

3. Try blending colors or even waiting for one color to dry and adding depth with a lighter or darker shade on top of it.

4. Once you're happy with the painting, set it aside to dry according to package instructions.

5. When your painting is dry, use a black marker to outline the picture.

Handprint Cactus

I love this craft because it not only makes for a pretty picture that you will have to frame, but it saves that tiny handprint of your child as a memory forever. Don't forget to write the date on this one, so that you won't forget at what age that little handprint was made!

A hand that is ready to get dirty!
Paint (I used green, yellow, and red)
Paintbrush
White cardstock
1 cotton swab
Black marker

1. Paint a generous amount of green paint onto the child's palm and fingers with a paintbrush.

2. Press the painted hand firmly onto the cardstock. This step can be done more than once if need be.

3. Allow the handprint to dry, and then dip a cotton swab in yellow paint and dot on flowers! I used yellow for the flowers and added a red center.

KEEP IT CREATIVE!

A Handprint Cactus also makes for a great greeting card for a teacher, friend, or family member. Do the above steps on the front of a folded piece of cardstock and add a clever saying like "Hands down, you are the best Grandpa around!" or for your teacher, "Thanks for helping me grow!"

4. You can also use a cotton swab to add some depth to your handprint by dotting lighter shades of green onto the handprint.

5. Once the handprint cactus is completely dry, use the black marker to add the cactus thorns.

Fancy Bandages

Make boo-boos a little better with a fancy Band-Aid. Oh, and another plus—this is a great craft for getting rid of fabric scraps!

Scissors
Fabric scraps
Band–Aids
Double-sided sticky tape (I love Elmer's Tape Runners!)

1. Cut a rectangle of fabric that completely covers your bandage.

2. Cover the top of your bandage with double-sided sticky tape.

3. Place the fabric on top of the bandage.

4. Turn the bandage over and cut off the excess fabric.

Snow Paint Snowman

My high school best friend, Annie McBroom, is a mother of two, a Montessori preschool teacher, and a great source for fun kid craft ideas! Kids will love that snow paint is 3-dimensional and feels and looks like real snow—especially if they live in a place where they rarely see snow! For this craft, Annie shows you how to make a snowman, but snow paint works great to make anything white and fluffy, including polar bears, clouds, or ice cream!

Shaving cream
White glue
Plastic spoon
2 sheets of colored paper (I used blue and purple)
Sequins, rhinestones, buttons, beads, glitter
2 (3–5") twigs
Pencil
Scissors

1. Mix together 1 part shaving cream with 1 part white glue. You want the shaving cream to maintain its fluffiness, so don't overmix. A quick 30- to 60-second mix with a plastic spoon will do the trick.

2. Dip the plastic spoon into the "snow" and make a large, 5" circle at the bottom of your paper.

3. Add 2 more spoonfuls that decrease in size to create the middle and top sections of the snowman. Don't be afraid to smooth out the snow with the back of your spoon or even your fingers!

4. Decorate your snowman (or snowwoman) with buttons, glitter, beads, or rhinestones. Don't forget to add a twig to each side of the middle section for arms. To do this, all you need to do is gently place them on top of the "snow"!

5. Finally, to make the snowman's hat, use a pencil to draw a 2" square on a piece of colored paper. Then draw a 2½"-long rectangle directly underneath the square to represent the brim of the hat. Next, cut the hat out and press it into the "snow" on the snowman's head!

KEEP IT CREATIVE!

You can transfer the snow paint to a sandwich bag, and then snip off one corner of the bag and pipe snow paint onto paper!

Monster Feet

Monster feet are the perfect addition to your kid's dress-up box! You never know when inspiration for a "Monster Mash" dance will strike. Kids will love making these silly feet and then wearing them too!

Scissors
Tissue paper and/or magazine pages
Decoupage medium
Paintbrush
1 (6") square of cardboard
2 large rectangular tissue boxes (with opening on the top of the box)
Tape

1. Cut tissue paper and/or magazine pages into 1" squares. Depending on how much of the tissue box you want to cover, you will need between 20–50 squares per box.

2. Use your decoupage medium and a paintbrush to glue the squares to the tissue paper boxes, making sure they overlap.

3. Cut 6 (5"-long) triangles out of cardboard to use as claws for the monster feet.

4. Use scissors to cut 1 (4") horizontal slit into the front of each of the tissue boxes. Insert the cardboard claws into the slit one at a time. Once 3 triangular claws are inserted into the slits on each foot, fold the remaining portion of the claw down inside of the tissue box and secure with tape.

Chapter 5

GARAGE

If your garage is anything like ours, it is filled to the brim with who knows what! The lawn mower, bikes, and baby stroller are about the only things I can find on demand, which is why I am going to encourage you and the kids to venture out to the garage now and hunt down some of the awesome craft loot hiding out there. In this chapter, you'll learn how to make crafts out of common materials found in your garage—golf balls, paintbrushes, and more! Sandpaper is probably my favorite garage crafting material. Can you believe that you can actually print children's crayon drawings on fabric with sandpaper? In addition, paint stir sticks become a portable tic-tac-toe set, bubble wrap turns into jellyfish, and rakes make rainbows. This chapter is full of fun surprises that your kids are guaranteed to love!

Flip Catch

This is a craft and game in one that kids will love playing over and over . . . and it's small enough to keep in a bag or car to play anytime. Your child can see how many times he can catch the balls without dropping them to the ground. It's harder than it looks!

Duct tape
2 plastic cups (the short punch cups work great)
Hot-glue gun
1 paint stir stick
8 cotton balls

1. Use tape to decorate the plastic cups. I kept mine very simple, and just wrapped 2 pieces of colored duct tape around each cup.

2. Heat up the hot-glue gun and put 1 nickel-sized spot of glue on the flat end of the paint stir stick. Place 1 plastic cup on the spot of glue. Turn the stick upside down, and attach the second cup to the other flat end of the paint stick the same way you did the first.

3. To make the balls, smash 2 cotton balls together and wrap a piece of tape (I used duct tape) around both cotton balls multiple times. Repeat these steps to make all 4 balls.

4. Now it's time to play Flip Catch! This game can be played by 1 person by placing the balls in one of the cups and trying to flip the paint stir stick over to catch the balls in the other cup. Count how many times you can catch 1 ball in a cup before they all fall to the ground! In the 2-player version, both people do the same thing and the winner is the one who catches the most balls after 3 rounds!

Tic-Tac-Toe

Tic-Tac-Toe is a fun crafty game that is great to take on the go. You and the kids can tic-tac-toe it up on camping trips or in the park, or can even enjoy a quick game on the sidewalk. All you need are 4 paint stir sticks, a permanent marker or two, and a few items from nature to use as your game pieces! Cheers to tic-tac-toe-ing on the go!

Permanent markers (I used black and blue)
4 paint stir sticks
5 dark colored rocks and 5 light colored rocks

1. Use the markers to make shapes, designs, and doodles on each of the 4 paint stir sticks. Make each stick the same or all 4 different. I made all 4 sticks different—1 with diagonal black and blue stripes, 1 with black and blue stars, 1 with multiple black triangles, and the last stick with horizontal black stripes.

KEEP IT CREATIVE!

You can use almost anything as game pieces. Rocks are typically very easy to find outside, but consider using keys, toy cars, leaves, coins, candy, cereal, or pieces of paper as game pieces. You could even use a little paint to make your own personalized set too!

2. On a flat surface, lay the 4 paint stir sticks out in a tic tac toe grid with 2 sticks placed horizontally and 2 sticks placed vertically on top of each other.

3. Use your rocks as game pieces and take turns adding one game piece to the grid. The winner is the first one to get 3 in a row and, in our house, the loser always gets to go first on the next round!

Nest Feeder

Instead of feeding the birds food, this feeder helps birds make nests. After you and the kids make this craft, be on the lookout for colorful nests in your neighborhood. The kids (and birds) will love this craft equally!

Paint stir stick
Permanent markers (I used red, orange, and green)
Clear plastic strawberry container with label removed
About 100–200 (3"–7") yarn and string scraps

1. Decorate a paint stick with the markers. Be sure to color the sides of the stick too!

2. Fill the strawberry container with 3-7" scraps of yarn, reserving 1 piece for the final step.

3. Turn the container so that the lid is on the bottom and loop 1 scrap of yarn or string through the existing holes in the bottom of the container to create a hanger.

4. Insert the decorated paint stick through the space that is created between the top of the lid of the strawberry container and the basket.

5. Take a piece of yarn and tie the strawberry container shut. Then hang and enjoy!

Sandcastle Magnets

Building sandcastles is always fun, and this craft allows kids to do just that without even making a trip to the beach! It's also a fun way to reuse old advertisements or save-the-date magnets. If you don't have any old magnets on hand, you can purchase adhesive-backed magnet sheets for less than 3 dollars at your local craft store. One 5" × 8" magnetic sheet and half of a piece of sandpaper will make one really awesome sandcastle.

Sponge brush
Glue
1 (5" × 8") magnet
1 sheet of sandpaper
Scissors

1. Use a sponge brush to apply glue to the top of your 5" × 8" magnet. Then place the sheet of sandpaper on top of the magnet. Allow to dry according to package directions.

2. Once the glue is dry, cut the excess sandpaper off so that you have a single 5" × 8" sheet of magnetic sandpaper.

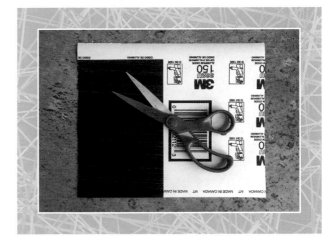

3. Now use your scissors to cut the sandpaper magnet into sandcastle pieces! I cut the 5" × 8" sheet of sandpaper into 5 (3" × 1") rectangles, 4 (4" × 1") rectangles, and 10 (1") equilateral triangles. You and the kids can cut your sandpaper into whatever shapes you would like. Then it's time to build sandcastles on the refrigerator!

KEEP IT CREATIVE!

This is a great craft to take on road trips or even while running errands. You can place the sandpaper magnets on a metal cookie sheet (not aluminum; it is not magnetic) and the kids can build sandcastles in the car!

Sandpaper Cactus

This Cactus is a super-fun touch-and-feel craft for kids! It uses an empty toilet paper roll and tape to form the cacti planters, and the actual cacti get their rough feel from sandpaper. These little potted cacti would make a great addition to the Race Track in Chapter 3 or would look great just sitting on a window sill in the kitchen.

Scissors
1 toilet paper tube
Cereal box
Pencil
Duct tape
Marker (I used green)
Sandpaper

Black marker
Single-hole punch
1 sheet of colored paper (I used orange)
Glue
Rocks or dirt

1. Use your scissors to cut a toilet paper tube into 3 smaller tubes of equal size.

2. Disassemble your cereal box by gently ripping the seams on the side and bottom of the box with your finger. Then, use the end of the toilet paper roll as a stencil to trace a circle onto the back of the cereal box. Trace 3 circles with a pencil and cut each one out.

3. Now it's time to assemble our 3 toilet paper tube pots. Place each circle on the bottom of the toilet paper tube section and wrap duct tape around each section. Use scissors to cut 6 slits in the duct tape. Then fold the duct tape over the top of the roll to secure the bottom of your pot and fold under the roll to secure the cardboard circle.

4. Use a green marker to color in the rough side of half a sheet of sandpaper.

5. Cut 3 different kinds of cacti out of the sandpaper. For one cactus consider cutting out 3 ovals. For the second cactus, cut out 3 finger-shaped pieces. For the third cactus, use a pencil to draw your version of a cactus and cut it out! Then, use a black marker to draw spines on your cacti.

6. Use a hole punch to punch 5 orange dots out of colored paper, then glue them to one (or all) of your cacti.

7. Assemble your cacti by placing a few small rocks in each of your 3 pots, then sticking 1 sandpaper cactus in each pot. Then fill each pot up with a few more rocks.

Awesome Fact

Elephant cactus can easily grow to be 60 feet tall. That's about as tall as a 6-story building!

Fabric Printing

Sandpaper is such a versatile crafting tool, and now I'm going to show you how you can use it to print your very own picture on fabric. It's true! You can draw anything onto sandpaper with crayon, and make it magically appear on any cotton T-shirt or bag with just an iron.

Crayons (I used blue, green, orange, and yellow)
Fine sandpaper
Scissors
Cereal box
T-shirt
Thin dishtowel or paper towel
Iron

1. Use crayons to draw a simple picture with very thick and dark lines on the rough side of the sandpaper. Then cut out the image.

2. Flatten and insert an empty cereal box into the T-shirt to keep the image from bleeding through to the back side of the shirt.

3. Place the sandpaper image-side down on the T-shirt, and put a thin dishtowel or paper towel over the top. Set the iron on a cotton setting and iron the image for 60 seconds. Pick up a corner and peek to make sure that the image has transferred to the fabric properly. If not, iron for 30 more seconds.

4. To set the color, remove the sandpaper and set a clean paper towel or dish towel over the image and iron on the same heat setting for 30 seconds. Wash and dry before wearing for the first time. I recommend washing the T-shirt separate from other clothes for the first wash.

KEEP IT CREATIVE!

Keep in mind that the image will be reversed when ironed onto the T-shirt, so letters and numbers need to be well thought-out. If you are using letters or numbers, hold your crayon drawing up to a mirror to make sure the letters will be reversed properly.

Paint Chip Mobile

Picking a paint color is always a big dilemma in our house. If you have the same problem, now you can turn those would-be wasted paint chips into material for a craft project with the kids! This is a fun, colorful piece that can be hung from a wall or ceiling anywhere in your home.

Acrylic paint (I used yellow)
Paintbrush
1 (12") stick
6 paint chip cards
Scissors
Single-hole punch
70" of string, cut into 7 (10") pieces
Clear tape

1. Use acrylic paint and a paintbrush to paint your stick. Allow the stick to dry completely.

2. Paint chips come in a variety of sizes, so use what you have on hand! I cut the paint chip cards into varying sizes between 2"- and 6"-long rectangular pieces.

3. Decide how you want your mobile to hang. Do you want the colors to go in rainbow order? Lightest to darkest? Or random? I created 6 strands, each with 2–6 rectangular paint chip pieces attached. Try arranging your cut-up paint chips on the ground in a similar layout.

4. Punch a hole in the top and bottom of each paint chip, except the bottom of the ones that will be the last paint chips on each strand.

5. String your paint chips onto a 10" piece of string through the holes punched into each chip.

6. Lay the string on the table and secure each paint chip with a small piece of clear tape on the back center of each chip.

7. Repeat steps 5 and 6 for all of your paint chip strands.

8. Tie each strand to your painted stick. Then, take your final piece of string and tie it to both ends of your stick to make a simple hanger.

Easter Basket

Give a plain brown cardboard box a new life and turn it into a personalized Easter basket! All you need is a cardboard box, a pair of scissors, a little rope, and a paint pen. Best of all, when Easter is over and the eggs have been hunted, you can recycle your basket—or save it for next year!

Scissors
Cardboard box (Note: The size of your cardboard box will determine the size of your Easter basket, so choose wisely!)
Ruler
Pencil
24" rope
Markers or a white paint pen

1. Use scissors to cut off the 4 flaps of your cardboard box.

2. Use a ruler to find the center on both of the long sides of the box and mark the center with a pencil. Use scissors to make a small slit at your center mark on both sides of the box. These marks should be centered both horizontally and vertically. This is where the basket's handle will go.

3. Slide one end of your rope through the slit in the basket, then tie a knot on the end inside the basket. Next, pull the rope through the other side of the basket and tie another knot.

4. Use a paint pen, markers, or paint to decorate the outside of your box.

Plant Markers

These simple garden markers will help kids (and adults) learn what plant is what. And remember—they don't just have to be used to mark herbs and veggies! Make a few plant markers to learn the names of bushes, flowers, and trees in your yard. Lantana, crape myrtles, and nandina are tricky words, but if the words are seen with the plants and heard every day, kids will remember them in no time.

Paintbrush
Acrylic paint (I used pink, orange, green, yellow, and blue)
5 paint stir sticks (or 1 per plant)
White paint pen

1. Use a paintbrush to paint 1 coat of paint on the top 5" of each of your paint stir sticks.

2. Allow the paint to dry according to package instructions, and then use a white paint pen to write the names of the veggies and herbs in your garden or the name of the plants in your yard.

3. Stick the garden markers in their places and watch your garden grow!

Golf Balls

Who knew golf balls could make such a fun, unusual canvas for crafting with kids! This is the perfect kid-made gift for the golf lover in the family! It's as simple as drawing on golf balls with permanent marker. The kids will love that Dad can actually use the golf balls they make him, and Dad will love that his lost balls are easier to find!

Permanent markers (I used green, light blue, dark blue, orange, yellow, purple, and black)
Golf balls
Brown paper bag (optional)
Rubbing alcohol (optional)

Gather up your permanent markers and doodle on your golf balls! Dots are fun to make since the golf balls provide nice round little spots to color. Straight lines and letters are a little trickier, but it's fun to explore patterns, colors, and the process of creating on this unusual canvas. I suggest doing this on top of a brown paper bag or newspaper. But keep in mind that rubbing alcohol takes permanent marker off of most things.

Awesome Fact

Did you know that the first golf balls were made out of wood? And there are at least 2 golf balls on the moon! Alan Shepard hit both of these golf balls at the end of the *Apollo* 14 Mission on February 6, 1971.

Bubble Wrap Elephant

Kids are so intrigued by the largest mammals living on land . . . elephants! This elephant craft shows you how to make a bubble wrap paint roller that gives any canvas a fun, spotted texture. Use it to make this awesome elephant, but also encourage the kids to think about other things to create—such as cityscapes, modes of transportation, or space scenes—using this fun new crafting tool!

Scissors
Bubble wrap
Tape
Clean paint roller
Gray paint

3 thin paper plates
2 pieces of white paper
Glue
Black marker

1. First, cut a piece of bubble wrap the same width as your paint roller. Then tape the bubble wrap around the roller.

2. Pour a little gray paint onto a paper plate and roll your bubble wrap roller in the paint. Do a test roll with the roller to get a feel for the amount of paint and pressure you will need to make a nice bubble wrap print. Paint 3 paper plates and 1 piece of white paper with the roller. Set aside to dry according to package instructions.

3. While you are waiting for your items to dry, cut 2 banana shapes out of white paper to be used as tusks, and 2 (2"-long) ovals to be used for eyes.

4. Once the painted paper products are dry, use scissors to cut 1 paper plate into as large an oval as you can. This will be the elephant's head.

5. Attach 1 round paper plate with glue to each side of the elephant's head.

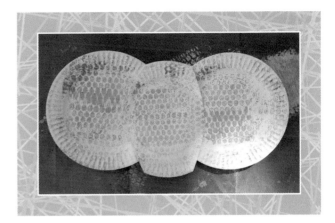

6. Cut the painted piece of paper into 3 equal strips vertically. Glue 2 strips together, to make 1 long strip. Accordion-fold the strip in pleats. This will be used as the elephant's trunk.

7. Fold over the top strip on the trunk and add glue to the painted side of that first strip. Attach the elephant's trunk to the center of the lower third of the oval-shaped paper plate. Then attach the 2 banana-shaped pieces directly underneath the elephant's trunk.

8. Use glue to attach the elephant's eyes to the upper third of the oval-shaped paper plate. Then use a black marker to draw 2 round black dots to act as pupils for the eyes.

Bubble Wrap Jellyfish

Your kids are guaranteed to love crafting these mysterious creatures that live in the deep blue seas. From bubble wrap to pipe cleaners to paint and more, this project puts your creativity to the test and lets you and your kids have oceans of fun along the way!

Scissors
Cardboard box
12" x 12" sheet of bubble wrap
Paintbrush
Paint (I used light blue, dark blue, and green)

Scraps of ribbon, yarn, straw, and pipe cleaners
Tape
Glue

1. Use scissors to cut off one side of the cardboard box. I cut a 10" × 12" piece, but you can make this piece of art as big or as small as you would like depending on the size of cardboard boxes you have on hand and how many kids will be making a project.

2. Cut your bubble wrap into 3" × 3" squares, then use a paintbrush to paint the bubble wrap and stamp it onto the cardboard. I used 2 different shades of blue to make the water.

3. Let the bubble wrap stamp dry according to package instructions, and then use a paintbrush to make a green seaweed at the bottom of your cardboard. I painted 3 (6"-tall) curvy lines that started at the bottom of the cardboard to resemble seaweed.

4. Cut 3 half circles out of bubble wrap to use as jellyfish bodies. Since all jellyfish are different shapes and sizes, each of my bubble wrap semicircles is a different size. My semicircles are anywhere between 2" and 4" tall and 3" to 6" long.

5. Now it is time to make the jellyfish tentacles! Each of my 3 jellyfish have 6–8 tentacles. Cut random pieces of string, yarn, ribbon, straw, and pipe cleaners about 5" long. Lay the tentacles onto the cardboard in 3 separate groups and use clear tape to tape each group down in a straight line.

6. Use glue or tape to attach the 3 jellyfish bodies over the taped tentacles and onto the cardboard.

Rainbow Rake

This Rainbow Rake is one of those crafts that is fun to make and even more fun to play with! And who doesn't love a rake that makes chalk rainbows on the ground in one swoop? So if you're stuck dealing with the age-old "I'm bored" blues, grab some clear packing tape, a rake, and sidewalk chalk and things are sure to look up!

Sidewalk chalk (The size of your rake will determine how many pieces of chalk you need as you place a piece of chalk in every other space in the rake. I used 5 pieces of sidewalk chalk.)
Rake
Clear packing tape

1. Place the piece of sidewalk chalk in the rake, allowing 1½" of chalk to stick out from the end of the rake. Cut a 15" piece of tape and wrap the piece of tape around the chalk and rake.

2. Repeat with the other 4 pieces of chalk, making sure that the tops of the chalk pieces are the same height.

3. To use the rainbow rake, just hold the rake as you normally would, and with minimal pressure drag the rake in a straight or curved lined to make rainbows!

Chapter 6

NATURE

To make the projects in this chapter, you and your kids will have to step out into the great outdoors for some "free" materials, including rocks, sticks, leaves, and trees! You'll combine these outdoor materials with staples such as permanent markers, toilet paper rolls, scissors, and more. And, while most of the projects in the book so far have left the type of tape, glue, or paint to use up to you, in this chapter you'll find a good number of crafts that call for acrylic paint, since it holds better to things like metal keys, rocks, and sticks. So lace up your tennis shoes, apply some sunscreen, and get ready to combine crafting with nature!

Texture Painting

To get this craft started, you and the kids have to step outdoors. Collect 5–10 various objects that can be pinched by a clothespin—things like leaves, grasses, or, if you're really lucky, a bird's feather! Once you're done gathering, come back to explore your newfound paintbrushes. If it's rainy or snowing, or you don't feel like going outdoors, you don't have to use just nature items. Feel free to explore the whole house for "paintbrush" materials.

Paint (I used red, but you can use as many colors of
 paint as you'd like)
Egg carton
3—5 clothespins
Anything that you don't mind getting painted! (Cotton
 balls, leaves, grasses, creatively cut pieces of paper,
 feathers, bread——the possibilities are endless!)
Painting surface (cereal box, cardboard, printer paper,
 newspaper . . .)

1. Pour different colors of paint into an egg carton.

2. Use a clothespin to pick up an object of choice.

3. Dip the object into the paint and then dab or smear the object onto your painting surface. Make patterns, create pictures, or just experiment with texture painting! Then allow the paint to dry according to package instructions and hang and admire your work on the fridge.

Emoji Faces

These Emoji Faces give you an opportunity to encourage your kids to think outside the box. Consider asking them to think about what other "free" round materials emojis could be made out of. What about old CDs, pumpkins, or even the frosting on cookies? Use whatever you have on hand to create this super-fun project because emojis rock!

Yellow paint pen (or acrylic paint and paintbrush)
Rocks (I used 5 flat, round or oval rocks)
Black permanent marker
Red permanent marker

1. Use a yellow paint pen to draw and fill in a large circle that covers the top of a rock. Give the paint at least 30 minutes to dry to the touch.

2. Once the yellow face is dry, it's time to make the emoji expressions! There are lots of options here, so just pick a few of your favorites and use black and red permanent markers to mimic the icons on your phone!

3. Once your faces are finished, use them to spruce up any garden space!

Hot Rocks

As a child, I would use crayons to draw on my backyard rocks all summer long. These are fun to make and, once the crayon melts to the face of the rock, they're even more fun to give as gifts! Wrap hot rocks up with the Brown Bag Gift Wrap from Chapter 2 and attach a fun note saying something like "Grandma rocks!"

Oven
Cookie sheet
Aluminum foil

6 rocks (smooth rocks work best, but feel free to explore all textures of rocks)
Crayons

1. Preheat the oven to 250°F.

2. Line a cookie sheet with aluminum foil and place rocks on the cookie sheet. Put the pan in the oven for 15 minutes.

3. While the rocks are in the oven, have the kids tear the paper off of the top of the crayons they want to use for this craft.

4. Once the rocks are heated, carefully transfer the aluminum foil to a spot that can handle hot surfaces.

5. Without touching the rocks with your hands, hold the crayon to the hot rock for a few seconds until the crayon starts to melt and become drippy. Then, explore how the crayon writes and draws on the hot rocks. If the crayon starts to get waxy looking, it's time to reheat the rocks! Feel free to reheat the rocks as many times as needed.

KEEP IT CREATIVE!

If you don't have a lot of smooth rocks in your area, this might be something to consider collecting while camping or on vacation to save in the craft box for a rainy day.

Garden Rocks

This craft is not only fun to make, but makes a great gift for the gardener in your life! If the kids are giving these garden markers as a gift, consider giving the recipient a white pen with blank garden markers so she can write the names of whichever plants she has growing in the garden! I'm positive that you and the kids will love making and using (or gifting) these adorable garden markers!

Rocks (I used 5 flat rocks that were big enough to write on)
Acrylic paint (I used green, blue, pink, red, and yellow)
Paintbrush
White paint pen

1. Paint each rock a different color with acrylic paint and a paint-brush. Each rock will likely need 2 coats of paint. Then set all of the rocks aside to dry according to package instructions.

2. After the rocks are dry, use a white paint pen to write the names of the plants in your garden onto the tops of the rocks. Then place them in your garden next to the assigned plant.

KEEP IT CREATIVE!

You can also use this technique to create vacation rocks! Whenever you go somewhere special, spend a few minutes or hours of hunting for the special rock that represents where you are in the moment. Then, when you get home, use a white-out pen or white paint pen to write the location from which the rock came. It's a free souvenir from a special place, and your kids will enjoy hunting for the rock and looking back and recalling happy memories from the places you traveled together.

Turtles

With this project, slow and steady wins the crafting race as your kids easily turn rocks into turtles. I choose to doodle turtles, but you can actually draw anything with permanent markers on rocks. Beavers, koala bears, beagles? Jets, astronauts, planets? Rocks are blank canvases and your markers are ready to make your kid's creative dreams come true!

Permanent markers (I used light green, dark green, and
   brown)
Rocks (I used 5 flat, smooth rocks)
White-out pen

1. Use a green permanent marker to draw a large circle that covers the top of a rock. Then fill in the circle with the green marker. Allow a few minutes to make sure that the marker is dry to the touch.

2. Then use a brown permanent marker to add 4 legs, a tail, and a head to the green circle you drew in the previous step. The legs are brown semicircles and should be added to the top and bottom sides of the circle. The head should be added to the top of the green circle and the tail should be added to the side opposite the head.

3. To make eyes, use a white-out pen to add 2 dots to the turtle's head.

4. Decorate the turtle's shell with brown or green permanent markers. You can make "X" shapes, plaid, polka dots, or any other fun designs you dream up!

Awesome Fact

Did you know that the largest turtle is the leatherback sea turtle, and it can weigh over 2,000 pounds? Just for reference, an average cow weighs 1,000 pounds!

Stick Mobile

Taylor Urban at *www.taylormadecreates.com* created this super-fun Stick Mobile that will make a statement hanging from the ceiling or on any wall. These mobiles are easy and free to make with things you can find around your house and in your yard. All you will need is a few good sticks, paint, string, and a drill. You'll have an awesome statement piece to spiff up any room in no time!

6 sticks (You need 1 large 6"—8" stick to act as your hanger and 5 smaller 4"—5" sticks to hang from the mobile.)
Newspaper
Acrylic paint (Taylor used white and a variety of blues)
Paintbrush
Paper plate
Drill
60" of string

1. Set your 6"–8" sticks on top of newspaper, and use acrylic paint to paint each stick. I decided to paint my sticks in an ombré fashion. To do this, pour a large circle of blue paint onto a paper plate. Use the blue paint to paint the first stick. Then add 1 nickel-sized circle of white to the blue paint and mix. Use this color to paint the second stick. Then continue this pattern until all 5 sticks are painted. You don't have to use the ombré technique; consider painting each stick a bright solid color, or even add stripes or polka dots.

2. Use a drill to drill 1 hole through the top of each of the 5 sticks that will hang from the mobile. Use a drill bit that is just a little larger than the string you will string through the sticks.

3. Use your drill to drill 1 hole into each side of the large stick you will be using as the hanger. Thread a 20" string through one of the holes on the stick and tie it to attach it to the stick. Then take the same string, thread it through the second hole, and tie it to secure it in place.

4. Now it is time to assemble your mobile! Take a 6" piece of string and string it through the hole in the top of 1 stick. Tie the string in a loop and knot around the hanger stick. Do this for each of the 4 remaining sticks.

KEEP IT CREATIVE!

You can opt out of using a drill and simply tie the painted sticks to the larger hanging stick. Just tie a simple knot around a painted stick and attach it to the hanging stick with another knot.

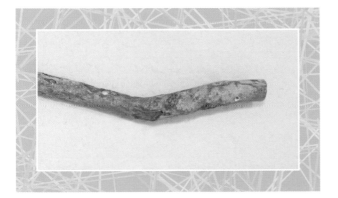

Key Wind Chime

This is a craft that gives back on windy days! You and the kids will enjoy listening to the sweet sounds of the keys chiming after you've crafted up this "free" creation!

Paintbrush
1 (12"–14") stick
Acrylic paint (I used yellow)
Paint pens (I used blue, orange, and yellow)
6 keys
String (cut into 6 (14") pieces and 1 (8") piece)

1. Use a paintbrush to paint the stick with yellow acrylic paint. Then set it aside to dry according to package instructions.

2. While you are waiting for your stick to dry, use your paint pens to paint one side of each of the keys, then set them aside to dry according to package instructions. Once the paint has dried to the touch, paint the other side of the keys and set them aside to dry.

3. Once all 6 keys are painted, tie a key to the end of a 14" piece of string and then tie the string around the stick. Repeat this for all 6 keys and all 14" pieces of string.

4. The last thing you need to do is make a hanger. Tie the 8" piece of string into a loop and loop it around the twig.

Stars

This patriotic craft is perfect for Memorial Day, Flag Day, Independence Day, Election Day, or Veterans Day! The kids can make stars out of any size twigs or sticks in your yard and rubber bands. The stars can be displayed on their bedroom wall, or even on a tree or a fence. These would also make great Christmas tree ornaments.

> 15 sticks (You need 5 (6") sticks, 5 (4") sticks, and 5 (3") sticks)
> 10—14 rubber bands
> 30" of string, cut into 3 (10") pieces
> 3—7 twist ties

1. Lay out 5 similarly sized sticks in the shape of a star. Try different sticks in different places; sometimes one with a tiny bend works better in one place than another.

2. Take your rubber bands and wrap them around the spots where the various twigs connect. The first connection is easiest to make using a rubber band. Continue connecting the twigs in the shape of a star with rubber bands and string. Twist ties work really well with smaller-size sticks, but they are not long enough for the thicker sticks.

3. Repeat with the second and third sets of similarly sized sticks until you have 3 stars in various sizes.

4. Use string to connect the stars to one another. Tie one end in a knot around the top of the smallest star and tie the other end around the bottom of the medium star. Do the same thing to attach the medium star to the large star. To make a hanger, tie the last 10" piece of string to the top of the large star, and hang your stars with pride.

KEEP IT CREATIVE!

A fun addition to this craft would be to paint the sticks! Stripes would be especially fun, or stars and stripes would be fitting on national holidays. Use acrylic paint, which will adhere best to the sticks, and allow the sticks time to dry before attaching them together!

Ice Towers

Ice towers are large chunks of ice with small toys frozen inside, and kids (and dogs) love them! They are fun and easy to make, but even more fun to play with outside on a hot summer day. Kids will have fun stacking the towers to build a larger tower and discovering the toys as the ice towers melt away in the sunshine!

3 plastic cups

Water

5—10 trinkets per ice tower (You'll need items that sink and float: rocks, cut-up straws, and even piece of fruit are all good options. The trinkets just need to be small enough to fit inside your plastic cups.)

Scissors

1. Fill each plastic cup with water to about 2" from the top of the cup.

2. Drop the 5–10 trinkets into each cup.

3. Stick the cups in a safe spot in the freezer and give them 4 hours to completely freeze.

4. After the water is frozen, take the plastic cups out of the freezer and use scissors to snip the top rim of the cup and down the side of the cup. This will allow the plastic to easily slide off, and free your ice towers.

KEEP IT CREATIVE!

While you are crafting the ice towers, consider talking to the kids about making predictions. As you are adding the trinkets to water in the plastic cups, ask the kids, "Do you think this item will sink or float?"

5. Take your ice towers outside and be prepared to get wet! Kids can stack the towers like blocks or even have a competition to see who can make their ice tower melt the fastest. There are endless ways to play with this fun craft!

Bird Feeder

This is the absolute easiest bird feeder to craft with kids. You'll need just 4 things: an empty toilet paper roll, peanut butter, birdseed, and a tree branch! I love that the hanging method is built into this bird feeder. Just slip the toilet paper roll over a low-hanging branch and have fun watching the birds enjoy their treat!

A dull knife
Smooth peanut butter
1 empty toilet paper roll

Birdseed
Low-hanging tree branch

1. Use a knife to spread a thin layer of peanut butter onto your empty toilet paper roll.

2. Next, use your hands to sprinkle birdseed onto the peanut butter covering the roll. Feel free to use your hands to push the seed into the peanut butter if you're having trouble getting enough to stick. The roll should be thoroughly covered with birdseed.

3. Find a low-hanging branch that is thin enough and sturdy enough to hang your bird feeder. Just slip the paper towel roll directly over the branch, and watch the birds enjoy your crafty treat!

Caterpillar

Rachel Hinderliter at *www.linesacross.com* crafted this adorable caterpillar with leaves! She uses a round paper punch to cut circles out of leaves, but you can easily use a plastic milk jug cap as a stencil and cut out the circles with scissors. As adorable as this caterpillar is, though, he's made of natural materials and won't last forever, so be sure to take a picture!

10 large leaves (you may want to play around with a few different kinds of leaves to see which work best)
1" round paper punch (optional)
Lid from 1 plastic milk jug (optional)

Scissors
Handful of grass
Glue
1 piece of paper (Rachel used white)
2½" pebbles, plus more if desired

1. Punch circles in the leaves with your paper punch, or use a milk jug cap as a stencil and cut the circles out with scissors. You will need 10 circles to make the caterpillar. Save the stems to be used as antennae at the end!

2. Use scissors to trim the pieces of grass that you found in the yard so they're each approximately 2" long.

3. Make a line of glue across your piece of paper about 4" from the bottom of the paper and 2" from the right and left ends of the paper. Start attaching pieces of grass to the glue line leaving about one blade of grass width in between each piece of grass. These will be the caterpillar's legs.

4. Start gluing the leaf circles on top of the caterpillar's legs. Glue the first circle down on the right-hand side of the paper, on top of the last legs. The next circle should overlap about ¼ of the first circle. Continue this pattern for 9 circles.

5. When you get to the end of the legs, glue 1 more leaf circle slightly above and to the left of the others to make the caterpillar's head.

6. To make the antennae, cut 2 of the stems from the leaves and glue them to the top of the caterpillar's head about 1" apart. You could also use twigs or more grass for this. Be creative!

7. Use glue to attach the 2 pebbles to the caterpillar's face to make the eyes.

8. Add pebbles, grass, twigs, mulch, more leaves, or anything interesting you find in nature to the bottom of the paper, underneath the caterpillar, to make the ground.

String Obstacle Course

This is another one of those "really fun to make, but even more fun to play" crafts! You will need 2 strategically placed trees (or lamp posts or stop signs or columns or chairs) and a ball of yarn. After the web is strung, the object of the game is to try to get through the course without touching a strand! But for younger kids, just trying to get through is fun, too. Let the games begin!

1 skein of yarn
2 trees
Scissors

1. To start the obstacle course, wrap the yarn once around the trunk of 1 tree and secure it with a knot.

2. Next, walk with the yarn ball in hand to the second tree and wrap the yarn around the trunk. Continue wrapping the yarn around the trunks of the trees until you and the kids are satisfied with your web! Make sure to wrap the yarn high and low. Typically 5–7 wraps is adequate.

3. There are multiple ways to play with the obstacle course, but for older kids, it's fun to see who can make it through without touching the "lasers"! For younger kids, it's fun to step over and under the strings and just make it through with a high five at the end!

Nature Names

This is a craft that can be completed anywhere in the great outdoors and it's a great activity for little ones who are antsy watching their older siblings play soccer or baseball at the field or even when they're just hanging out in the backyard with a friend. Of course, this craft can be completed inside as well. This is also a fun way to introduce sorting and classifying like objects to kids. Any craft that sneaks in a little learning is one of my favorites!

Twigs (optional)
Leaves (optional)
Grasses (optional)

Rocks (optional)
Berries (optional)
Pinecones (optional)

1. Ask your kids to sort the objects they've collected either by color, shape, size, or whatever else they can think up.

3. If you want this craft to be more permanent, consider using glue and tape to secure each object to the back of a cereal box or cardboard!

2. Have the kids write their name with the nature items they collected. Siblings can work together to create one name with the nature items, say their last name. Or the kids can work individually to create a Nature Name with just their first name. You can make a letter out of just one nature item, say rocks. Or you can use multiple items to create one letter, like the "E" in the picture above is made out of leaves and pinecones. Don't forget to snap a picture once this project is done, since these outdoorsy items won't last forever!

KEEP IT CREATIVE!

Before you start this project, have the kids round up a few nature items. Ask the kids to gather things such as different colored leaves, a small branch from a bush, grasses, and rocks of different colors. Pinecones, berries, and flowers are good additions too.

U.S./METRIC CONVERSION CHART

VOLUME CONVERSIONS

U.S. Volume Measure	Metric Equivalent
⅛ teaspoon	0.5 milliliter
¼ teaspoon	1 milliliter
½ teaspoon	2 milliliters
1 teaspoon	5 milliliters
½ tablespoon	7 milliliters
1 tablespoon (3 teaspoons)	15 milliliters
2 tablespoons (1 fluid ounce)	30 milliliters
¼ cup (4 tablespoons)	60 milliliters
⅓ cup	90 milliliters
½ cup (4 fluid ounces)	125 milliliters
⅔ cup	160 milliliters
¾ cup (6 fluid ounces)	180 milliliters
1 cup (16 tablespoons)	250 milliliters
1 pint (2 cups)	500 milliliters
1 quart (4 cups)	1 liter (about)

WEIGHT CONVERSIONS

U.S. Weight Measure	Metric Equivalent
½ ounce	15 grams
1 ounce	30 grams
2 ounces	60 grams
3 ounces	85 grams
¼ pound (4 ounces)	115 grams
½ pound (8 ounces)	225 grams
¾ pound (12 ounces)	340 grams
1 pound (16 ounces)	454 grams

OVEN TEMPERATURE CONVERSIONS

Degrees Fahrenheit	Degrees Celsius
200 degrees F	95 degrees C
250 degrees F	120 degrees C
275 degrees F	135 degrees C
300 degrees F	150 degrees C
325 degrees F	160 degrees C
350 degrees F	180 degrees C
375 degrees F	190 degrees C
400 degrees F	205 degrees C
425 degrees F	220 degrees C
450 degrees F	230 degrees C

LENGTH CONVERSIONS

U.S. Length Measure	Metric Equivalent
¼ inch	0.6 centimeters
½ inch	1.2 centimeters
¾ inch	1.9 centimeters
1 inch	2.5 centimeters
1½ inches	3.8 centimeters
1 foot	0.3 meters
1 yard	0.9 meters

INDEX

Note: Page numbers in *italics* indicate craft projects.

ABOUT THE AUTHOR

JAMIE DOROBEK is the creator behind the popular craft, parenting, and lifestyle blog *CreatingReallyAwesomeFreeThings.com*—or *C.R.A.F.T.* She has been blogging full-time since 2012, and has worked with brands from The Home Depot to Target to Elmer's to Mod Podge to Martha Stewart Crafts, Command Brand, and many more. She and *C.R.A.F.T.* have been featured on Apartment Therapy, Design*Sponge, *Craft Business* magazine, *The Meredith Vieira Show*, and the *Huffington Post*, among others.

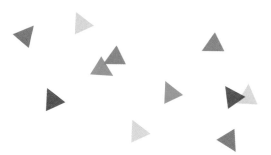